Just. Plain. Stupid.

by Curtis Walker

Just. Plain. Stupid.

Table of Contents

Preface

This is an entirely true story, though some names of places, people and organizations have been changed. Specifically, David Coleman, the main character, is a pseudonym, and the email address I have used, david82@FreeAMail.net, is fictitious and does not correspond to any known user, domain or email service.

In the Beginning

Sunday, August 18

David Coleman, whoever he is, is awfully persistent. And a slow learner.

It was about a week ago that I first got an email from Snapchat asking me to confirm his email address. Or make that *my* email address. Except that I never signed up for Snapchat. Coleman did. So after checking that this wasn't some sort of scam, I clicked on the "not me" link to remove my email address from the account. But the next day, he tried again. This cycle repeated itself about a dozen times over the next few days, so since he wasn't getting the hint, I tried another angle. This time, I confirmed the email address, then used the "forgot password" link on Snapchat's site to reset the password and lock him out of "his" account. For good measure, I later logged in and chose the option to delete the account, which they said would happen in 30 days. Hopefully now, he'll get the hint.

Monday, August 19

Sadly, David Coleman isn't getting the hint.

Which is going to make it pretty tough for him to find a job because he keeps signing up with recruiters using my email address, none of whom had the decency to ask for verification before spamming me. From the emails that have been flooding in, he's looking to drive a truck, but he's also interested in general labor and there was a position as a merchandising assistant that came up as a match. According to the job description, the incumbent will be responsible for the total merchandise operation in the office; will support all daily operations within the department, which will ultimately affect company sales, gross margin and weeks of supply objectives; will work with vendors in developing solid relationships to effectively resolve various issues; and will assist the merchandising manager with day-to-day functions. The ideal candidate will be detail-oriented with a college degree and strong PC proficiency. Since he can't seem to figure out what his own email address is, he hardly qualifies as "detail-oriented."

With most of them, I was able to unsubscribe to the alerts easily enough, but with one of them, like Snapchat, I had to reset the password to get into the account he created so I could turn off the email alerts and ultimately delete the account.

From reading his profile, he lives in Deland, Florida, and he's looking for work in the Miami area. He's not going to get anything until he gives his own email address instead of mine. He'll figure it out soon enough when he doesn't get any responses.

Tuesday, August 20

David Coleman still hasn't figured it out.

Today, he used my email address to create accounts with two online banks, neither of which saw fit to wait for the address to be confirmed before firing off all sorts of spam. Welcome, terms and conditions, stuff like that. Helpful hints on how to use their online banking system. It might be something I would appreciate if I were their customer. But I'm not. Sadly, that little detail doesn't seem to interest them.

Wednesday, August 21

David Coleman is back on the job hunt.

This time, he applied with a place called Initiative Trading and, once again, gave my email address to them. From checking into them online, they seem like a shady outfit. Might even be a scam. Then again, he appears to be desperate. That, combined with his stupidity, might make it a good match.

Hi David,

I am Jim Dennis, one of the Recruiters at Initiative Trading. Thank you for completing your application for consideration as one of our newest traders. With over 20 years in business, we still get excited to see who will be our next trader at Initiative Trading.

I will be personally reviewing your application. While I am doing that, please take the next step in the application process and watch a 48-minute video from our head traders at Initiative Trading. The video should be viewed as soon as possible and in its entirety since it contains useful information about our hiring process.

After you have viewed the full video, you will be directed to another page of frequently asked questions and asked to provide the best telephone number and time to be contacted. I will then contact you typically within 2-3 business days to schedule a suitability interview, where you and I will finalize the recruiting process.

If you have any questions, please contact me directly, but please know that I cannot schedule your suitability interview until you have watched the above video in its entirety.

I look forward to speaking with you.

Best regards,
Jim Dennis
Trader | Recruiter

Thursday, August 22

Looks like David's application is moving forward. If only he knew.

Hi David,

Thank you for completing your Initiative Trading interview request. As a Recruiter, it is my job to discover if you will be a great fit for Initiative Trading and vice-versa (that is, if Initiative Trading will be a great fit for you).

You can expect to be contacted by me via telephone or e-mail in the next 2-3 business days to schedule your suitability interview.

There is no need to prepare for the interview — simply be yourself. Your personality and personal drive are more important to us (and your success as a trader at Initiative Trading) than your past accomplishments or how well you communicate. Ideally, you should have access to a computer and the Internet during the interview.

In a prior e-mail, we asked you to watch a 48-minute video that contains useful information about our hiring process. If you have not had a chance to watch that entire video, please take the time to do that now since I cannot schedule your suitability interview until you have watched the video in its entirety.

Coleman probably hasn't watched the video, since he never got the email, but for interest, I watched a bit of it. A couple of young hotshots run the operation and to get started, you have to put $5,000 of your own money into a sub-account and they add $20,000 of their own, giving you the seed money to trade stocks in the hopes you'll make a profit, which they take a percentage of. They sell you on the fact that you're getting the backing of an entire team that will train you and help you along the way, something you wouldn't get if you just set up an online account yourself. It still seems shady. Whatever the case, how this idiot is going to come up with five grand is a mystery since he's not going to be able get a job until he figures out what his own email address is.

Friday, August 23

Today, I got an email from Larters Bank, one of the banks David Coleman signed up with earlier in the week, saying that his debit card is on the way. How nice of them.

Checking into this business with Coleman a little more, I searched online to see if there are any good hints and tips I hadn't already thought of to try to get him to stop using my email address. It's apparently a common problem, more so than I realized. Someone posted a story about another guy signing up to Ebay and ordering stuff, forcing him to call them to block the account. Someone else posted about a guy filing their income tax return with H&R Block and requesting information from a whole bunch of colleges. Then there was a post about someone who used his address to sign up to Instagram and subsequently found out that the guy ordered a case for his iPhone, is interested in a new Ford pickup truck and signed his child up for a Scholastic education account.

They did advise trying to contact the guy, which I could, if only I knew how.

But unfortunately, aside from what I've already done, there's not much else you can do about it. It's not a technology problem, it's a human problem. And this human definitely has a problem. Surely he's got to realize, after all the stuff he's signed up for without getting a single response, that something's wrong.

One additional thing they did advise was to have a strong password and use two-factor authentication for your email account, both of which I have, just in case Coleman tries to access it, as he seems to genuinely believe it's his.

Monday, August 26

David Coleman is still on the warpath.

Today, he requested information from Liberty University. Affordable study options are available for their accredited online college degrees, they say. Hard to imagine he'd get through their program since he's failing the first question – what's your email address?

Tuesday, August 27

Unable to find work or get information on educational programs, David Coleman is now looking for solace online.

So he signed up with MatchSniper, a dating site. Find a hookup contact in your neighborhood, they say. And they're filling my inbox with alerts for new girls in Miami. Alerts like the one telling me that 28-year-old chumba-wumba viewed his profile. She's single, has an average body type and blonde hair. Evidently Coleman thinks that if he keeps giving my address to these places, persistence will pay off and he'll eventually start getting the emails.

Sadly, they wouldn't send a password reset link, which would allow me to go in and turn off the alerts and delete the account, so I had to add them to my blocked senders list.

Wednesday, August 28

Today, Larters Bank sent me an email asking David Coleman to activate his debit card.

Too bad they didn't ask him to confirm his email address before creating the account.

Friday, August 30

Today, David Coleman signed up to get a quote on a fleet card for his grass cutting. Whatever that is. From the looks of things, he's spending more time smoking his grass than cutting it.

The responses keep flooding in from his inquiries about getting grants for schools in his area. Maybe it's just as well he's not getting them since they wouldn't do him much good anyway. As they say, you can't fix stupid.

Monday, September 2

David Coleman seems to have stopped looking for a job for the time being, but he's still on the education track.

Today, I got this from Almond Education:

Hello David,

I wanted to be the first to Welcome you to Almond Education.

My name is Allison, and it is my privilege to manage your benefits towards the best education possible.

You will now have exclusive access to all school related benefits.

We specialize in helping our members get the education the way they want, in their desired time. If that means finding flexible course schedules, online study options, or local campuses, we can do it.

Stay tuned, because we have a lot in store for you!

Thanks!

Allison K.
Account Manager
Almond Education

And the first lesson begins by learning what your email address is.

Too bad Coleman keeps skipping school.

Wednesday, September 4

Just when I thought the job stuff was tailing off, I got an email for David Coleman to confirm an interview at Target.

Larters Bank also sent me another email reminding Coleman to activate his debit card.

I wonder if it's dawned on that guy yet why he's not hearing back from all these places.

Friday, September 6

I got another email today asking David Coleman to confirm the Target interview.

Target must be getting pissed.

I know it's tough to recruit people for low-paying retail jobs, but they don't know how lucky they are that Coleman didn't give them his own email address.

Saturday, September 7

Today, David Coleman signed me up for weather alerts for the Miami–Dade County area.

There's a lot of weather activity in Florida.

But there sure isn't much going on between his ears.

Monday, September 9

Having struck out with MatchSniper a couple of weeks ago, David Coleman tried three more dating sites today.

From the profiles, he's black, 5-foot-6 and 190 pounds, was born on November

5 and is in his early 30s. He says he's looking for a long-term relationship, and on his "about me" page, he states, "Like going out and having sex." He also uploaded a selfie. Not surprisingly, he doesn't look like the brightest guy, nor a great catch for any woman looking for a suitor. It gave me the shakes just looking at his spaced-out mug. He's got a bushy, unkempt salt-and-pepper beard and mustache and must have taken the shot in a dark, narrow hallway. He's got a big forehead, and there sure can't be much behind it.

There are women out there who don't know how lucky they are that Coleman can't even figure out what his own email address is.

He also signed me up for a site called Surveys and Tests, where they pay you to take surveys. Except that you need to get the email in order to be able to take the surveys. Something he can't do until he gives them his own address instead of mine.

Wednesday, September 11

Another day, another new site that David Coleman signed me up for.

This time, it's WorkSiren. A hiring specialist emailed me saying that Coleman was looking at a Dollar General job. As if I cared. Coleman obviously doesn't either, since he hasn't bothered to ask himself why he hasn't gotten any replies to all the sites he signed me up for.

Friday, September 13

David Coleman has switched back to the education track.

This time, he asked for information from Florida Career College and Kilton University.

If at first you don't succeed, try, try again.

He also got another reminder from Larters Bank to activate his debit card.

This has gone on for a month now. And he still hasn't figured it out.

Tuesday, September 17

David Coleman really wants to get on Snapchat.

The very day they deleted the first account he created under my credentials, he created another one. And he was so frustrated over the fact that he didn't get the email confirmation that he asked for it to be sent three times. It didn't occur to him that it's not Snapchat's problem that he doesn't know what his own email address is.

This time, rather than delete the account as I did previously, I confirmed the email and reset the password, leaving the account there so he can't try this again. Let him keep banging away until he figures it out.

Wednesday, September 18

Today, David Coleman tried to sign up with Varo, another online bank.

Fortunately, unlike the last two, Varo sent a verification code to the email address he provided (mine), with a two-hour expiration that he has to enter before he can create the account. Who knows, maybe this time he'll get the hint. Then again, there seems to be thicker material between his ears than the concrete and steel holding up Hoover Dam.

Thursday, September 19

David Coleman wants information on becoming a motorcycle technician.

But before he learns how to fix motorcycles, he needs to fix his brain.

Assuming he has one.

Do you want to turn your passion for bikes into a career?
Demand is growing for professional technicians!

Thank you for requesting more information about the technician training programs of Central Florida Motorcycle Institute. You've taken the first step on the road toward an exciting career as a technician in the motorcycle industry.

I'll be in touch soon!

If you prefer to call me, you can reach me at (786) 555-4271.

Roberta Sedaris

Sunday, September 22

It's been a busy day for David Coleman.

For starters, there were two more online dating sites, neither of which had the courtesy to ask for email verification before spamming me, forcing me to log in and delete the accounts. From the profiles he created, he stated he likes to give women head. With the first site, unable to verify his email address with them, he did so with his phone instead. So he knows there's a problem, yet he still keeps hammering away using my email address in the vain hope it will magically start working if he keeps quoting it over and over again. This guy really is a special kind of stupid.

Later in the day, he signed up with Netspend, a provider of prepaid debit cards. Or at least he tried to. Like Varo, they sent him (me) a passcode that expires in five minutes before he can create an account. It was a passcode he never got. Then he asked for another one. He didn't get that one either.

Next was Florida Unemployment Claims, a nongovernmental agency that sent him (me) a guide on how to apply for benefits. Soon after, he signed up at American Hope Resources. A search revealed that it's an online community for hardship sufferers where like-minded people going through similar struggles offer resources and moral support in your time of need. He needs help all right, but there's no cure for stupidity. Finally, he signed up at Mammoth Awards & Savings.

Tuesday, September 24

Money matters have moved to the top of David Coleman's agenda.

He tried to open up a checking account with Bank of America, but today, I got a notification that he was turned down.

Update on your account application

DAVID JULIAN COLEMAN,

We received your recent application for the listed product(s). However, based on our records, we're unable to open new deposit accounts for one or more applicants.

Bank of America Advantage Plus Banking™ Account

For your privacy, we don't share details in this email of why we were unable to fulfill your request online.

We appreciate your interest in our products. If you have questions about this decision, you can call Risk Identification Support Center Customer Service.

Thank you for considering Bank of America for your financial needs.

Next, he tried to sign up with Melio Payments, a service to pay bills with bank transfers, debit cards and credit cards. But alas, like Netspend, he had to enter a passcode they sent me before the account could be activated. Undaunted, he tried again with Varo, who again sent me a passcode. Finally, he requested information from BMO Harris Bank.

Give him an A for effort.

But an F for brains.

Friday, September 27

Banking issues continue to command David Coleman's attention.

Stymied at his attempts to activate his Larters Bank debit card via email, he was able to do it through his phone, something Larters was kind enough to tell me today. Shortly thereafter, he tried to use the card for a 15-cent charge at Samsung. It was declined because that's 15 cents more than what's in his account. Larters was also nice enough to send Coleman's postal address and phone number to the unverified email address he had given them (mine). This is a bank that states on its website that it offers serious security. Our bank-level security protects your sensitive personal information and prevents unauthorized use, they say. Right. If this is how they handle security, perhaps I'm doing Coleman a favor by unwittingly obstructing his access to them. Regardless of how it affects me or him, it's disturbing to see any financial institution operating this way.

At the bottom of their emails, Larters always states I'm getting them because I'm a Larters customer who agreed to their electronic communication agreement. No, I didn't. Coleman may have agreed to it, but I sure didn't.

Moving on, he signed up for another outfit that issues prepaid Mastercard and Visa cards. With this one, I reset the password on the account, unsubscribed from all emails and also changed the phone number on file so he won't be able to use it to regain access to it. It will also prevent him from ever activating the Angry Birds card he ordered. Maybe that will get through to him. He then tried to sign up with Lili Financial Services for a debit card, but he struck out again since they sent me the email he needed to complete the setup procedure.

To say the least, Coleman must have terrible credit, since he keeps going to these obscure places. Bank of America, the only major brick-and-mortar bank he's tried, turned him down flat.

Before winding up the day, he signed up at Employment Assistance and I had to get myself out of a couple of additional dating sites he signed me up for.

This is getting out of hand.

Saturday, September 28

It was another busy day for David Coleman online.

Which made it an equally busy day for me.

He started things off by signing up for updates on a WordPress blog about how mental health can be improved through physical activity. Fortunately, they insist on email verification, unlike Larters. It's a sad state of affairs when a WordPress blog handles email subscriptions with more consideration than a bank.

Adding to the "his credit is in the crapper" theory, I got this from Capital One:

More on your credit card application decision

David, unfortunately we were unable to approve your application at this time. We know you're disappointed. To help you understand why, we've explained the reason for this decision in a letter or email that you'll receive within 10 days.

Later in the day, I got an email as to where to get that letter. But sadly, I had to enter a password that was the last four digits of his social security number, date of birth and five-digit zip code. I've got the latter two, but not his social. At least not yet. Darn. I'd like to know why he was rejected, although I can readily figure it out.

No doubt these money problems are depressing him. Who could blame the guy? So that's probably why he headed back online and signed me up at another dating site. Like the other sleazy sites he signed up for, they don't wait for email activation before spamming the heck out of me, forcing me to log into the account and delete it. I didn't even have to reset the password this time, since they were kind enough to send the password (1982Dodge) in the email. So now at least I know where he picked up the "82" of my email address, david82@FreeAMail.net. As for the Dodge part, maybe that's where he was conceived. Or born in. Maybe both. Whatever the case, I'm probably doing these women a favor by deleting the account since Coleman isn't exactly a prize catch. He's unemployed, the keyboard I'm typing on probably has better credit than he does and he's dumb as a bag of rocks.

After doing a little research online, I found that he lives in a hovel that looks like something the Big Bad Wolf could blow down with a good puff. The appraised value for the 1,039-square-foot home is just under $59,000, but personally, I wouldn't give him more than $59 for the place, as it sure hasn't aged well since it was built nearly 60 years ago. On a positive note, there's a bus stop right out front. He probably needs it since I doubt he can afford a car. Among the known past residents is someone named LaToya Washington-Coleman. A background search on her showed she's living at a different address with a different phone number, and from her LinkedIn profile, she's been a beauty consultant for Mary Kay for the last six years. Probably Coleman's ex. She was smart to dump him, but you have to wonder about someone who would ever get involved with this guy in the first place. Maybe what triggered all this with Coleman is a divorce or separation. He got his own phone number complete with a new email address that probably happens to be close to mine and is going to town building himself a new online identity.

Monday, September 30

First thing this morning, David Coleman was back on the rampage.

Unable to rub two quarters together, he began looking for a loan. He first applied for a Discover Student Loan, with predictable results.

Dear DAVID COLEMAN,

Thank you for your recent request for a Discover Loan. After careful consideration, we are unable to approve your request at this time for the following reason(s):

INSUFFICIENT INCOME

As a reminder, your credit score will not be impacted by your request since we used a soft credit inquiry to check your eligibility.

Please contact us should you have any questions. Please include your name, address and reference number.

Sincerely,

New Accounts
Discover Personal Loans

Next he tried a place called Expansion Capital Group.

David,

This is Kelly Powell with Expansion Capital Group. I have your incomplete funding application in front of me and need to confirm some of the information I've received. Give me a ring at your earliest convenience, so we can have a quick chat to determine how best to proceed.

Best Regards, Kelly Powell | Business Funding Manager

After that, he applied for another checking account, this time with TD Bank, who were kind enough to inform me that his application was incomplete. Not that the end result would likely have been any different if he had filled it in completely.

Still feeling lonely, he signed me up at four more dating sites.

He sure isn't giving up very easily.

Tuesday, October 1

David Coleman tried again with Varo.

Much to Coleman's chagrin, they're one of the good guys and insist on email verification before proceeding.

Up yours, you idiot.

Wednesday, October 2

Overnight, David Coleman signed up for another dating site.

Once again, they sent me the password, the same one he used at the last dating site, which enabled me to go in and view his profile. This time, he uploaded another selfie and filled in some personal details about himself. He drinks occasionally, smokes socially, has a high school education (I don't believe it), lists "other" as his religion and has four children. Now there's a scary thought, as Coleman's genes aren't exactly a gift to the human race. He says his ideal date is a woman who already has kids, is good with kids, wants more children and smokes. He says he loves sex and is looking for one-on-one dating, online friends, swingers, alternative activities or just online flirting. He's not particular. He's just lonely. And stupid.

Interestingly, Coleman also claims to be employed. Well, maybe he did get a job after all. Or more likely, he's just lying. After all, an employed moron living in a hovel who has four kids would sound much more attractive to a potential mate than an unemployed moron living in a hovel who has four kids.

But alas, he'll never know, since I changed the password and deactivated the profile.

Hours later, I had to do it all over again with yet another site.

He's persistent, I'll give him that.

Thursday, October 3

David Coleman signed up for another service to pay bills through an app and a personalized Visa debit card.

Except that he can't use it since he had the verification code sent to me instead.

So I logged in and reset the PIN, and since they require the sign-in code they send via email, he'll never be able to get in. For shits and giggles, I also changed his name to "Ass Hole." Later in the day, I finally found the link to close out the account completely and got a confirmation that my email address had been unlinked from the account.

Looking more into this guy online, I found his Facebook profile, where he's pictured with who I presume is one of his kids. He likes motorcycles and claims to have been a mechanic for several years, working on brakes and tune-ups for motorcycles, dirt bikes and ATVs. He also listed the name of the high school from which he allegedly graduated 15 years ago (can you say "no-fail policy"?), plus his favorite movies and television shows. He's also a fan of hip hop music and the Miami Heat.

Of his more than 1,600 friends, all but a dozen are female, most of whom are posing in bikinis or other similarly skimpy attire. No doubt what's on his mind. In a way, it's sad. Here's a guy with 1,600 "friends" and is lonely. But it's not my problem. And filling my inbox with his shit isn't going to make him any more popular with members of the opposite sex.

Sunday, October 6

David Coleman wants to get on Instagram.

But he must not want to get on that badly because he's using my email address again.

Like Snapchat, they asked for an email confirmation, but instead, I used the "not me" link to remove myself from the account he created.

Tuesday, October 8

Just when I thought David Coleman might be starting to get the hint, he's back at it.

For starters, he tried signing up at Varo again. He'd have been able to if only he used his email address instead of mine. He followed that up by requesting another promo code from BMO Harris Bank for an Essential Business Checking account bonus. Then he signed up at NetWallet. Make all the right money moves, they say. Need objective advice, expert info and helpful tools to answer your money questions? Turn to us. Tell us more about you and we'll recommend things like the best credit card for your spending habits, simple ways to up your credit score and more. In their introductory email, they asked for email verification to be able to access the account online and through the app to receive credit monitoring notifications. With all I know about him, he sure doesn't need an app to tell him that his credit rating is shit.

Once again, this dumbass used his favorite password, so I was able to go in, turn off all the email notifications and change the password. I could have closed the account completely right away, but I figured it would be best to leave it there for a while and let him keep hammering away at it.

It is interesting to note that of all the places I've changed the password on accounts he's created using my email address, not once has he ever tried to get the password reset. I suppose you need to have a little brain power to figure out how to use a "forgot password" link, and it's brain power he doesn't have. He's got just enough to keep signing up with these places and not one bit more.

Wednesday, October 9

David Coleman went on another rampage today.

His first target of the day was IsMyGirl, flooding my inbox with pictures of girls posing in compromising positions. When I went into the account to change the password and stop the emails, I noticed that he didn't bother uploading his own picture. No doubt it was because he's always getting booted out of these sites for some mysterious reason he still can't figure out. Not long after that, he tried Varo for the fifth time.

Later in the day, he went to town and signed up at four more dating sites. I never knew there were so many of them. From one of the profiles he created, he says his four kids live with him. If that's true, I pity them. I can't imagine what kind of father this guy is. One thing's for sure, he's not spending a whole lot of time with them, as he's spending the bulk of his time online, mostly with those sleazy dating sites. What a great example to be setting for your children.

Marching On

Thursday, October 10

David Coleman doesn't give up easily.

Today, he tried signing up with Varo for the sixth time, then he went to another dating site filled with porno cams that asks you to download a .bin file when visiting their site. No doubt it's some nasty malware or spyware. I can only hope he's executed it and put it on his system. Maybe that will scare him off going online, because at this point, it seems like that's the only way I'm going to get rid of him.

Friday, October 11

More gifts from David Coleman in my inbox today.

No doubt following up on the credit card rejection, Capital One sent him (me) an offer to sign up for CreditWise, a service that gives free credit monitoring and personalized suggestions for improving your credit score. He doesn't need credit monitoring, he just needs credit period, as the good folks at Capital One are already aware. As for what he can do to improve it, well, that's going to be tough. Especially for an idiot like him. There was a similar offer from BMO Harris Bank right after the Capital One email. Capital One at least gave me the opportunity to unsubscribe, but BMO didn't, stating "you are getting this email because you requested to receive emails about our special offer." No, I didn't. Coleman requested it. And even if I had, I ought to have the right to ask them to stop.

At least all that didn't represent any new activity, unlike his seventh attempt to sign up with Varo.

The day seemingly isn't complete without Coleman signing up for another dating site, and once again, he didn't disappoint, making two attempts at WellHello. Your fun dating, hookup and swingers site with style featuring an online adult community that's designed for you to meet and hang out with like-minded singles and couples, they say. It doesn't matter if you're looking for one night of fun or a longer-term relationship – we've got what you want. We pride ourselves on being welcoming whatever your orientation or needs. We've got support online to make sure any questions or concerns that you might have are always taken care of. Whatever. But unlike most of the others, they actually insist on email verification before creating an account and spamming the recipient.

For good measure, I got a follow-up from a previous inquiry he made at Central Florida Motorcycle Institute.

From: Roberta Sedaris
Subject: Interview Questionnaire
To: David Coleman

David,

Training for a new career can be an exciting time and you may need some help getting started. I am here to help you get the information you requested but have not been able to connect with you by phone. Assuming that you have reviewed the information on our website and have looked over the brochures, I would like to give you the opportunity to take the next step to be considered for admission.

The next step is to complete your admissions interview, which will be used to determine whether CFMI is the right educational fit for you and how I can assist you with your career goals. The interview can take place over the phone or in person if you live nearby. However, I do need to schedule a time that works best for both of us.

To start, please click on the link below. It will take you to a preliminary interview questionnaire, which will only take 8 to 10 minutes to fill out. When completed, you are letting me know that you've reviewed the information and would like to continue moving toward your new career in the motorcycle industry. As soon as I receive your questionnaire, I can call you so we can set a time to talk.

David, I really look forward to helping you and talking with you soon!

Sincerely,

Roberta Sedaris

Don't bother following up, Roberta. If he can't figure out what his own email address is, he sure as hell ain't going to be able to fix a motorcycle.

Saturday, October 12

Something new from David Coleman today.

He created an account at SoundCloud so he can listen to free music and podcasts. Before deleting the account, I retrieved his listening history. His favorites were "The Golden Child" (YK Osiris), "Worth It" (YK Osiris), "INTRO" (Baby Jesus) and "Bandit" ft. NBA Youngboy (Juice WRLD).

Then he made a second attempt at another of those prepaid debit card places. But later in the day, he managed to order a prepaid Mastercard from them despite not being able to enter the passcode they sent me. Perhaps he did it with his phone, like Larters Bank. Yet I, not he, got the email notification even though the address has never been verified. My, what tight security they have.

David,

Welcome! Your personalized card will arrive in 7-10 business days. Once your card arrives, activate it and verify your identity.

Below are a few things you can do to prepare for your Card's arrival:

Online Account Center

Check your balance, create a budget, enroll in additional features, and so much more!

Anytime Alerts

Enroll in optional alerts so you're ready to receive updates about Card Account activity as it happens.

Take your money mobile so you can manage your account on the go.

I tried logging in to thwart his latest act of stupidity, but even though I had the password, they wanted the card number. Shit.

Monday, October 14

That motorcycle place is hot to get David Coleman as a customer.

Roberta Sedaris at CFMI sent Coleman another email offering a virtual tour of their campus along with various links and an invitation to call her. But sadly, Coleman was too busy at jerkmatelive.com. Never jerk off alone again, they say. He set up a live-streaming account there, but he can't use it until he activates it with the link they sent me. Poor guy.

Later in the day, he opted for something a little more tame when he signed up with Diner DASH Adventures, a game available from an app. He can play the game without confirming the email address, but he signed me up for updates. Thankfully, they sent a verification code he has to enter in his phone that I got and he didn't. In the email, they say, "Thanks for registering! We're so excited to have you join the wonderful and kooky world of DinerTown!" Right now, I feel like I'm in a real-life game of my own in the kooky world of ColemanTown.

Tuesday, October 15

The beat goes on.

Overnight, David Coleman tried signing up with Varo for the eighth time. He's also getting more into games as he signed up for a Nintendo account. Or at least he tried to. Sadly for him, Nintendo takes email verification more seriously than Larters Bank and sent him (me) a verification code that expires in 24 hours before he can proceed. In the email, they state, "If you do not know why you have received this e-mail, please delete it." I know why I got it, but I'll delete it anyway.

It had been a few days since he last signed me up for a dating site, but he got back into the swing of things on that front at BBPeopleMeet. Big and beautiful singles put BBPeopleMeet on the top of their list for BBW dating sites, they say. It's FREE to search for single men or big beautiful women. Use BBW personals to find your soul mate today!

Who knows, maybe he really could find his soul mate there. If only he could get it through his thick skull that my email address isn't his.

Wednesday, October 16

Unable to use his new Nintendo game, David Coleman is getting antsy.

Early in the day, he tried twice more to create an account with them. Then in the evening, he tried two more times. That makes five attempts over the last two days. One apparently needs an account in order to buy games for their Nintendo Switch console, a video game system that retails for between $200 and $300. So without an account, it's effectively a brick. Much like what's between his ears. How he was able to afford such a thing is a bigger question. This guy obviously doesn't have a dime to his name and no credit whatsoever. Maybe he got it as a gift. Or perhaps he stole it.

However, his anxiety isn't preventing him from trying to seek solace in dating sites as he signed me up for another one. The 23rd such site.

That guy is an awfully slow learner.

Thursday, October 17

David Coleman is growing increasingly desperate to create a Nintendo account.

But he's not desperate enough to use his own email address.

First thing this morning, there were two more attempts. Around midday, he tried twice more. And later, he tried five more times. For the record, that now marks 14 attempts in the last three days. Whereas he used the nickname "David" over the past two days, today he used "Dave" and later "Dave82." Yeah, that's going to make all the difference. At least I can take comfort that he's causing himself as much grief as he's been giving me. He must be a big gamer. Either that or it could be a birthday present for one of his four kids. Perhaps he should get one of them involved because they're probably more on the ball than their father. One of them, in fact, his son JaMarcus, was recently named Student of the Month at his elementary school, something his ex proudly shared on Facebook.

In between Nintendo signup attempts, he went back and inquired about programs with Kilton University after I unsubscribed following his first attempt with them.

Dear David,

Are you looking to jump-start your career? A degree from Kilton University can be a great way to get started or to build upon your existing education and skills. We provide a warm, friendly community with faculty and staff truly committed to your success.

Since 1968, Kilton University has maintained a practical, hands-on approach to career-focused education to help our students achieve their personal and professional goals in less time than you may think.

WHY KILTON UNIVERSITY
Degrees at the associate, bachelor's, master's, and doctoral levels
One class at a time schedule
Small classes taught by accessible, industry-experienced faculty
Real-world learning that can give you a competitive edge
Supportive, student-centered environment

Degrees offered in the fields of Arts and Design, Business, Chiropractic Medicine, Criminal Justice, Culinary, Education, Fire Science, General Studies, Health Care, Information Technology, Interdisciplinary Studies, Legal Studies, Nursing, Psychology, Sport Management.

In addition, he also got an invitation to their Halloween-themed Scare Fair Open House. But there's nothing scarier than a dumbass like David Coleman trying to get through a university program.

Meanwhile, even though he didn't sign up for any more dating sites, I still had to scrub messages like this out of my inbox:

From: JigglySister
Subject: JigglySister_is_checking_you_out
To: David Coleman

I'm just looking for a bit of naughty love. naughty and need to get off... I would very much like to go through this really soon Just need to feel some love again. contact me asap..

No, JigglySister, you really don't want anything to do with Coleman. Trust me on this. You don't know how lucky you are that he's not getting this email.

Friday, October 18

It was another busy day for David Coleman online.
And another busy day for me.
He tried again at WellHello, then he signed up for emails at City College.

Congratulations on taking the first step toward a brighter future! We've been teaching students like you since 1984, offering hands-on classes that are designed to be career-focused. At City College, you won't just read from a textbook. You'll learn real-life skills that you'll be using on a daily basis in your future career.

Our admissions and financial aid staff are here to answer all of your questions and provide guidance for your journey every step of the way.

A couple of hours later, I got a couple of emails from Credit Karma.

From: Credit Karma
Subject: Welcome to Credit Karma!
To: David Coleman

Welcome to the Credit Karma community! Whether you're here to build your scores or monitor your reports, we're ready to help.

A few things to keep in mind:
* Your membership will always be free (really!).
* You can update your scores and reports every 7 days, and checking Credit Karma will never hurt your scores.
* We offer credit monitoring and identity monitoring — and they're both totally free.
* Your security is our priority and we're committed to your privacy. We'll never sell your personal info to anyone for marketing purposes.

Happy to have you here!
The Credit Karma Team

From: Credit Karma
Subject: Access Credit Karma with Your Active Account
To: David Coleman

Hi David,

You're receiving this email because you began registering a new account, but you may already be a Credit Karma member.
Credit Karma only allows members to have one active account, so the new account you created has been automatically canceled. To access Credit Karma, please log in using your active account's email address.
If you forgot the email address or password you use for Credit Karma, you can quickly recover them via our lookup tools.

Cheers,
The Credit Karma Team

I suppose it was fitting "karma" that someone else already created an account with my email address to foil him. Unless he had created one himself previously and I didn't catch it. So much shit from him has been flowing through my inbox lately that I could have missed it. Whatever the case, his fixation on credit monitoring is just as puzzling as how, after all this time, he still hasn't figured out that he's using someone else's email address.

Then he turned back to Nintendo and made two more attempts to create an account there. Since it had been 17 hours since he last tried, I suspected he might have taken the unit back to the store and exchanged it for one that "works." But this one won't work any better than the last one did as long as he keeps giving my email address instead of his.

For the record, the Nintendo tally now stands at 16.

An hour after the pair of Nintendo emails, I got one from Domino's Pizza. He must need to refuel himself since signing up to all those websites can be exhausting. And there is a lot of him to refuel as he is packing a few extra pounds, something he always makes sure to mention on his dating site profiles. They sure didn't make it easy, but I finally removed myself from their email list, along with taking him off their text alerts as well. If only they would make it as difficult to subscribe in the first place.

Before the end of the day, he reached out to Southeastern Interstate University.

From: Lolita Fitchner
Subject: Lolita-SIU
To: David Coleman

Hello,
Thank you for spending time with me today, We got a great start. I provided some information below.

Thank you.

Lolita's program recommendation:
Bachelor of Business Administration specialization in Entrepreneurship
Bachelor of Business Administration specialization in Management

Thank You,

Lolita Fitchner
National Admissions Advisor

Not long after, he got an appointment with Lolita for tomorrow afternoon.

From: Lolita Fitchner
Subject: Appointment Confirmation – SIU
To: David Coleman

David,

Thanks for your interest in exploring how SIU can help you move your education forward.

I want to confirm that your appointment is set for Saturday, 10/19 at 2:00 PM. I look forward to discussing how earning a degree through SIU can help achieve your goals. Before the appointment, please take some time to:
• Learn more about SIU at our website
• Get answers to your Financial Aid questions

You can also review the information in our Admissions Center. You will need to login using the information below.
• User Name: David.Coleman

If you have additional questions before our scheduled appointment on Saturday, 10/19 at 2:00 PM just contact me for assistance.

Best Regards,
Lolita Fitchner
Admissions Advisor

Just to give him some grief, I logged in with the user ID Lolita provided, then set a password and answered the security questions as follows:

What is your mother's maiden name: Coyote

What is the name of your favorite teacher: Idiot

After this, I proceeded to add a bunch of fictitious information and changed his city to Athens, Georgia. What the hell, might as well have fun with this. If he doesn't give a shit, neither should I. If only there were a place to delete the account or cancel the interview.

Saturday, October 19

David Coleman remains a busy man.

Overnight, he signed up for two more dating sites. One was new and the other was his fourth attempt at WellHello. There must be something special about WellHello, though for the life of me, I can't understand what it could possibly be. Early in the morning, he signed up for yet another dating site, then an hour later, he tried signing up at N26, an online bank, only to be foiled by the inability to verify his (my) email address. He tried twice more a minute later, but again, both verification requests came to me and not to him. Obviously, he must still be having trouble finding a place to do his banking, further evidenced by his second attempt to open an account with Bank of America. Not surprisingly, the result was identical.

Update on your account application

DAVID JULIAN COLEMAN,

We received your recent application for the listed product(s). However, based on our records, we're unable to open new deposit accounts for one or more applicants.

Bank of America Advantage Plus Banking™ Account
Bank of America Advantage Savings

For your privacy, we don't share details in this email of why we were unable to fulfill your request online.

We appreciate your interest in our products. If you have questions about this decision, you can call Risk Identification Support Center Customer Service.

Thank you for considering Bank of America for your financial needs.

Part of me is beginning to feel sorry for him. He must think the world is out to get him. But only part of me. Two more dating sites followed, the latter was one of the two he signed up for overnight. The first time, I made the mistake of not changing the password first before deactivating the profile, but I didn't make that same mistake this time.

Moving on, he resubscribed to Domino's Pizza and Jobs2Careers emails, from which I had to unsubscribe again, and tried two more times with Nintendo, bringing the total to 18.

Sunday, October 20

It's still full steam ahead for David Coleman.

Overnight, he tried to reactivate a profile from a dating site he previously signed me up for and also signed up for a new one, forcing me to lock him out of both. What a shame that he won't get those messages from lara8232, chocmousse and XpamelaX88. But again, I'm probably doing them a favor.

I continue to be amazed as to how many of these dating sites are out there. He can sure find them. That much he has a talent for. Yet he can't figure out that he's using someone else's email address instead of his own.

Around midday, he signed me up at Hardtime Relief, a place that offers financial assistance for single parents, people with low income, seniors and folks with disabilities who qualify for help from various programs sponsored by the U.S. government, private entities and charitable organizations. He certainly needs help. But no government program can give him a brain.

Coleman still remains oddly fixated on his credit score, as evidenced by this email an hour later:

From: YourScoreandMore
Subject: David, Get Your Complimentary Credit Score
To: David Coleman

Dear David,

It's critically important to your finances to keep tabs on your credit score. You know that you're so much more than just your credit score - Unfortunately, it's the only tool lenders have to gauge your creditworthiness. To them you really are just a number.

While we can't change the game, we can help you play by the rules. We're offering a complimentary credit score and immediate access to your credit report when you start your trial.

Right now, Coleman is more than a number. He's a blithering idiot. An idiot who's driving me up the wall. If only I could easily change email addresses and be free of this moron. But I've had it for more than a decade and it's linked into some important places where I can't readily change it. Abandoning it just isn't a practical option. I have little choice but to defend it. But that's becoming a full-time job.

Sadly, he wasn't done for the day. He resubscribed to the Domino's list, made two more attempts with Nintendo, then in the evening, he applied with CBX

Expedited, a trucking company. The thought of Coleman behind the wheel of an 18-wheeler is about as frightening as it gets. The world can only hope there's some strict licensing requirements in Florida for big rig drivers. Stricter than just plucking a license out of a Cracker Jack box.

Monday, October 21

David Coleman continues to explore furthering his education.
Early in the morning came this from SIU:

From: Sandra Harrison
Subject: Login Information – SIU
To: David Coleman

David,
As we discussed, here is the Admissions Campus presentation link that will give you valuable information about SIU as well as a view into our Virtual Campus. Take a look and write down any further questions you might have for the next time we talk. I have also provided your log-on information below for the SIU Admissions Center.
• User Name: David.Coleman

Best Regards,
Sandra Harrison
Admissions Advisor

He obviously talked with them over the weekend and asked about his login information, which, of course, he never got. So again, I had a little fun and went through it a little more, changing his name to Daffy Duck and answering a few more questions stupidly before stopping at the point where they wanted his educational background. Maybe it will trigger something in a future conversation. Or not.

A couple of hours later came another marketing email from CFMI. At least they allowed me to unsubscribe, which I did. As I did at Domino's, which I had to do for the fourth time after Coleman resubscribed me. In the email, they said the coupons he's after are linked to the store and email, so he won't be able to use them.

My heart bleeds. For good measure, he tried four more times with Nintendo, bringing the total count with them to 24. As if he figured those attempts were going to go any differently than the first 20 did. Coleman obviously hasn't read the following article from Nintendo's support site regarding "not getting the email":

> *I did not receive an e-mail containing a verification code after I created a Nintendo Account. What should I do?*
>
> *Check your spam/junk email folder to see if the email is there.*
> *Make sure there are no filters in your email account that may be blocking emails from us.*
> *Make sure that you are entering your email address correctly in the account creation screen, and click resend verification code to have a new verification code sent.*
> *Try registering your Nintendo Account with a different email address.*

The last point is especially appropriate. Just substitute "different" with "your own."

Tuesday, October 22

I keep wondering why David Coleman keeps trying with those prepaid debit card places.

This morning, he made his fourth attempt at the most recent place he signed up with. No doubt he wants to activate the debit card he ordered. But seeing as though he has so little money and no job, he could just as easily put what little he has to his name in a shoe box. A very small shoe box.

Later in the afternoon, he made a momentous decision and signed up for a program at CFMI.

> *From: Roberta Sedaris*
> *Subject: CFMI Enrollment Agreement for David Coleman*
> *To: David Coleman*
>
> *Dear David,*

Congratulations on taking the next step in an exciting career in the motorsports industry.

You are currently enrolling at the CFMI - Orlando campus in the 42 Week Motorcycle Technician + FAST & Yamapro program. Prior to continuing your Online Enrollment Agreement process, please click the link below for information about our graduation rates, the median debt of students who completed the program and other important information.

Please click on the link below and fill out the Online Enrollment Agreement for CFMI. Before you begin, please make sure you gather the following information:

Three unique references with a full name, address, telephone number, and email address. Have your method of registration payment available.

Once you begin, you'll have 50 minutes to complete the process. If you don't complete the forms within this amount of time, you will be required to start a new session and begin the forms again, so please plan accordingly.

If you have any questions or need assistance, please don't hesitate to call me.

It would be nice to have his attention diverted for 42 weeks, but I'm not holding my breath that it's actually going to happen. You see, he actually has to go through the enrollment. And in order to do that, he has to get the email. Oh by the way, they actually require payment too. Which is pretty tough when you don't have a dime to your name and you can't even open up a checking account and have to resort to prepaid debit cards you can't activate because of your own stupidity.

An hour later, while waiting in vain for this email to arrive, he tried WellHello for the fifth time. Hey, might as well have some fun while you're waiting.

Later in the day, I got another email from Jim Dennis at Initiative Trading, who was probably following up from Coleman's earlier application.

Hi David,

Thanks for your recent interest in Initiative Trading.

We know there's a lot of conflicting information out there about Proprietary Trading and that sometimes it's hard to separate the wheat from the chaff.

If you didn't know, our CEO researched and wrote an in-depth White Paper on the Proprietary Trading industry: What is Proprietary Trading? The Complete Primer on Prop Firms. He discusses the industry's beginnings, its history, where it is today, where it's going, and key indicators to look for when researching a prop firm.

Whether you decide you want to trade with Initiative, find another prop firm, or trade on your own, we feel that you should be armed with the knowledge to make the decision that's best for you.

If you have any questions about the report, please feel free to contact me directly. I look forward to speaking with you in the future about trading with Initiative.

Even though he's missing out on these emails, it's probably for the best, at least as far as he's concerned. I don't think I'm going out on a limb by suggesting that trading stocks is a little out of Coleman's league.

It had been almost a full day since he last tried to create a Nintendo account, but he was back at it again late in the afternoon with his 25th attempt. What made this attempt different from the rest was that he used the nickname "Chillin" instead of some combination of Dave or David. It still hasn't occurred to him that the only thing he hasn't changed, the email address, is what's wrong.

In the evening, he tried again at WellHello and signed up to another obnoxious dating site that flooded my inbox without bothering to wait for the email verification. Celiar wanted to make friends. Nichola sent me a "sassy message." And I could upgrade my account to initiate dating with Nella. Gee, sounds tempting. But instead, I turned off the email notifications, then changed the password to lock him out.

Wednesday, October 23

David Coleman really wants to register for that motorcycle course.

But he can't.

Because he keeps quoting my email address instead of his own.

Around the noon hour, Roberta Sedaris forwarded the identical email she did yesterday. No doubt Coleman called her to say he didn't get the email and asked her to send it again. To me, and not to him.

Maybe when they talk again, Roberta will suggest trying a different email address. Maybe then it will click. At least I can hope.

Late in the day, however, what little optimism I had on that front faded when I got two more verification requests from Nintendo, bringing the tally to 27.

Thursday, October 24

Now David Coleman wants to put his stuff in storage.

> *From: Storage King*
> *Subject: Your move-in reservation*
> *To: David Coleman*
>
> *Hi David,*
>
> *We're glad to have you with us.*
>
> *Please be sure to arrive at least 30 minutes before closing time on your move-in date to make sure you have enough time to complete your rental. The location's office hours are:*
>
> *Monday - Friday: 9:30 AM - 6:00 PM*
> *Saturday: 9:30 AM - 5:00 PM*
> *Sunday: 9:30 AM - 5:00 PM*
>
> *What You'll Need at Move-In:*
> *A government-issued ID for paperwork*
> *A copy of this email (recommended)*
>
> *Reservation Details*
>
> *David Coleman*
> *Phone: (786) 555-7546*

Move-In Date 10/30
Space Details: 5'x10' Unit (50 Sq. Ft.), Outside unit/Drive-up access

Monthly Rate: $55.00
$1 First Month's Rent: $1.00
One-Time Admin Fee: $24.00
Total Move-In Cost: $25.00

Even though he can't complete the enrollment procedure at CFMI, this is probably an indication that he's still planning on an extended absence while he's on the course. I tried to go in and cancel the reservation entirely, but without that option available, I went ahead and changed his reservation date to November 21 and to a different location at the opposite end of town. I need to start going on the offensive here. I have to do something that will cause him plenty of grief and aggravation that he will hopefully associate with my email address. Then maybe he'll start using his own.

The rest of the day was mostly quiet. No doubt he was busy packing. But he wasn't too busy to make two more attempts with Nintendo. The total now stands at 29.

How thick-headed is this guy?

Friday, October 25

Before he goes away for the course, David Coleman is determined to create a Nintendo account.

He made five more attempts during the day, bringing the total to a mind-boggling 34.

And he *still* doesn't get it.

Saturday, October 26

This morning, David Coleman applied for a Mastercard Black Card.

At his request, they emailed me a copy of the terms and conditions. I wonder if he's aware of the annual fee of $495, which is about $495 more than his net worth. Then again, what does he care? The odds of him getting approved for it are somewhere between slim and none.

Of course, he might think they'll give him a Black Card because he's black. He is that stupid.

Tuesday, October 29

I was beginning to wonder if something had happened to David Coleman, since he hadn't signed me up for anything over the past couple of days.

But overnight, he tried two more times with Nintendo, bringing the total to 36.

He's alive.

But he's not well.

Wednesday, October 30

More overnight activity from David Coleman, who has been keeping some odd hours of late.

This time, he signed me up for an account at Nav.com. Get matched to the best financing offers, they say. Business credit and personal credit are extremely important for getting financing. See what you can get approved for today! Well, I don't exactly need to hack any credit reporting bureau's database to know that he won't get approved for anything. So it's just as well that I went in using his favorite password (he keeps making it so easy), turned off all the email alerts and changed the password. For good measure, I changed his address and phone number so that he can't get verified that way.

Thursday, October 31

The date of David Coleman's original reservation at Storage King came and went without incident.

The reservation that I changed to November 21 is still there. And he didn't actually move in, since there was no account on file with my email address. According to their website, they won't let you create one until you move in. Perhaps his well-laid plans with the school he was going to attend have gone awry.

Just to have a little more fun with him, I changed the reservation again, this time to November 1 and upgraded his unit to a small 6' x 7' cube, which costs $75 per month. See what happens.

Meanwhile, as he sits and broods in his hovel wondering why he's not getting the emails from the school and all the other places he's signed up with, I continue to be inundated with messages like this:

From: GoodCumber
Subject: GoodCumber added you to her favorites
To: David Coleman

willing to keep this brief nd sweet. im not able to really get out and meet people organically. To be honest right now I am just wishing to get some thrill. 28 year old gal curvy build 5'6 black color hair brown colored eyes. only wanting safe & clean fun with a mature man. Think you're down for it?
;)

For good measure, I went back to Snapchat and deleted the ghost account Coleman can't get into. Let's see if he tries going down that road again.

Friday, November 1

More goings-on with Storage King today.

Around the noon hour, I got a message from them saying he missed his reservation. But then, a few hours later, I got another notification saying that he updated the reservation for tomorrow at 4:30 pm. Coleman must have called them to change it, but he didn't change the unit or location.

Obviously, I hadn't made enough of an impression on him. So I screwed around with him a little more. More like screwing back, actually. This time, I changed the date to November 5, changed the unit size again and selected a location in Cincinnati. Enjoy the drive up I-75, asshole.

Maybe now he'll pay attention.

Or not.

Less than an hour later, he was back at it, this time with Online Schools. Perhaps he's soured on SIU, the place where I changed his name to Daffy Duck, and the motorcycle place he can't register with because he doesn't know his own email address.

What surprised me was the healthcare angle. How'd you like to have David "I love to give women head" Coleman tend to you in a hospital?

Saturday, November 2

David Coleman has become a night owl.

Around midnight, he signed up at Consumer Merchants, a place that touts itself as a hub of disability benefits guidance. Personally, I can't think of a greater disability than a missing brain.

From: Hillary Stevenson
Subject: You may qualify for Disability Assistance
To: David Coleman

Hello,

I hope that everything is going well. I just wanted to tell you that having a health issue is a very serious issue that should be addressed. You must be proactive and learn more about disability benefits.

At this present time, help is being given to people that qualify.

Please keep in mind that you must meet the requirements and follow the required steps to qualify. An experienced staff member can walk you through the entire process. This will help you save time, and help you avoid making crucial mistakes during the process.

You may not know it, but all American Citizens can get Social Security Disability if they meet the requirements. You should take out the time to get more information. You have everything to gain and nothing to lose!

Don't hesitate to ask questions. We are here to help you.

Sincerely Yours,

Hillary Stevenson
Social Security Disability Claims Specialist

Not more than a half hour later, he signed me up at VioletDates, the self-proclaimed best international dating site to meet singles. How kind of him.

From: VioletDates
Subject: David, pleeeease confirm your email ;)
To: David Coleman

Dear David,

Thank you for joining VioletDates

Confirm your registration and stay opened for love!

To make your search better and help you find a lifepartner, we thoroughly check every ladies' background, reputation and sincerity of intentions.

Minutes later, Alena visited his profile. Again, it was so nice of them to notify me even though I hadn't verified the email address. So again, I went in, changed the password, turned off all email notifications and finally, deactivated the profile. They were also kind enough to send along the password, as if I didn't already know it. In his profile, he used much of the same rhetoric as he's used in the past, but he listed his occupation as "Building." That he's building an occupation or that he works in a building? Whatever the case, I don't think either is true. He also uploaded a new picture. He's letting his beard grow, he's got goggles on top of his head and that piece of snot in his nose will surely attract any number of would-be eligible bachelorettes. The goggles are probably the ones he uses for motorcycle riding. Perhaps it's an indication that he hasn't given up on that motorcycle course in Orlando. But first, he needs to put his stuff in storage. And he's got a long drive up I-75 to Cincinnati.

Later in the day, I began to wonder what became of his Nintendo game. It had, after all, been a few days since he last tried to create an account. But just when I thought he may have taken it back to the store and finally given up or, God forbid, used his own email address, on cue, he tried twice more, bringing the grand total to 38 such attempts.

Stubbornness and stupidity are a lethal combination.

Sunday, November 3

David Coleman still wants to put his stuff in storage.

Late in the morning, I got a notification from Storage King saying that Coleman's reservation has been updated for tomorrow at 4:30 pm. Shortly thereafter, he changed it to 4:00 pm. Both, however, are still in Cincinnati. This time, I'll let him go through with it, or at least try to. Then, if he indeed moves in and creates an account, I'll really go to town. All I can do at this point is try to cause him enough grief so that he gets gun-shy about using my email address.

Happy Birthday

Wednesday, November 6

All quiet on the David Coleman front for the last few days.

Perhaps he had a big party for his birthday yesterday.

But just after the clock struck midnight, he was back in action.

First was this from eharmony:

Welcome!

You've successfully registered at eharmony. That means you're one step closer to finding a happy and fulfilling relationship. As part of the exclusive eharmony community, you have access to one of the largest networks of quality singles who are all looking for a meaningful relationship.

We recommend visiting eharmony regularly, as new members are signing up all the time. Our most active members have the highest chances of falling in love.

The whole eharmony team is here to help you find the right match who will bring even more joy into your life.

Then this from EliteSingles:

Dear new EliteSingles member,

We are pleased that you have chosen EliteSingles for your search for the right partner. By registering, you have already taken the first crucial step on the road to a lasting and fulfilling relationship.

To receive individual partner suggestions, please give us the opportunity to get to know your unique personality better, and to better understand your expectations for a relationship.

Take a few minutes to complete the free personality test and then receive your individual personality report and partner suggestions directly after.

The scientific personality test is the "heart" of the matchmaking process at EliteSingles.

The test tells us more about you, your wants and your needs, and allows us to identify exactly which members really suit you. Our personality test and extensive matchmaking experience enable us to offer you daily partner suggestions which are not only compatible with your personality but also correspond to your relationship expectations.

If you have questions about your dating on EliteSingles, please do not hesitate to contact our Customer Care team.

Yours truly,
The EliteSingles team

Sadly, both places forced a "personality test" on me before finally allowing me to delete the account. They asked everything but "How do you feel when websites don't require email verification before allowing you to create an account?"

Interestingly, later in the day, for the first time, Coleman used the "forgot password" link to try to get back into one of the dating sites he signed me up for a while ago. Too bad for him that I got the link instead.

Thursday, November 7

David Coleman is getting back into online dating again.

And he's getting particular with his tastes.

Overnight, he signed up for two dating sites where you can find sexy, plus-sized partners. He didn't upload a picture, but he stated he was looking for a woman aged 18-39. And he didn't beat around the bush when it came to what he was looking for. Just sex, not any of the other flirting or alternative activities he's checked off at other sites. And even though they say you won't get any notifications until you validate your email address, they send them anyway. Like the notification that haileeyMae44 viewed his profile. And that 39-year-old isabellapsn is seeking a man in his area. Going to keep perving on pics or tell me something about you, she asks? Along with the flirt from 51-year-old FtLauraDale.

Once again, not that I needed it, but those sites were nice enough to send me his password. Along with his IP address. So now I have the name of his ISP as well. As someone said to me recently, I know *way* too much about this guy. Far more than I ever wanted or cared to know.

I suspect this recent spike with the dating sites is because he has some time on his hands as it looks like the motorcycle course hasn't panned out. Not only has there been nothing more from them, but he hasn't moved in at Storage King either. In fact, he went as far as to cancel the reservation. No doubt he got royally pissed off with them for not emailing him the confirmations. As if it's their fault he doesn't know his own email address.

Then again, I didn't know his real email address either. So after a little searching online, I came up with a posting from him on a site listing potential scam callers in which he kindly gave his Yahoo address. Which could prove helpful.

> *david coleman*
> *i have a company or somebody thats calling my neighbors and giving them personal information about me to people that i dont know, i feel that if its something in regards to me you need to try to talk to me and not giving out my personal information there phone number is 6305557101*

So he's worried about someone else giving out his personal information, but he has no problem whatsoever sharing the intimate details of his life with a perfect stranger like me.

One has to wonder how he even has enough brains to use a computer or a smartphone.

Friday, November 8

David Coleman is like the Energizer Bunny. He just keeps going and going and going.

Overnight, he signed up at POF.com. Which stands for Plenty of Fish. Or in my case, Plenty of F---ing emails. When I checked my email first thing in the morning, there were 56 messages from those sleazeballs that I had to clean out of my inbox. Many were from users who were saying hello. Users like Boujieehippie, Helen_Norton55, Danielle_Young, PhukingFloyd, Zara_Doherty, Lucille_4274,

DerrySmith, PerfectBigSpoon27 and Londababy32. In addition, there were nine messages from users who want to meet him for reasons I can't possibly understand. Users like Lounder2, Onlyfun103, Ashleyafrare, Carverrx, Bethany82, Island_baby97, Peacefulmindss101, Marissa5670 and 2kylar.

So rather than simply log in and delete the account, I tried a different approach this time. Now that I have what I believe is his Yahoo account, I set that as the email address in the account and left the following description in the profile:

Hey Asshole, has it dawned on you why you haven't been getting any emails when you've been signing up at david82 (at) FreeAMail.net? It's because IT'S NOT YOUR EMAIL ADDRESS!!! Start using your own address instead. Then you'll find that all your Nintendo verifications, Roberta Sedaris' emails from CFMI and all your communications from these filthy sites will suddenly work!

Maybe that will work. Or not. But I have to try.
For interest, here's how he filled out his profile:

Describe your personality in one word: Athletic
I am looking for: Long term
Intent: I want a relationship.
Longest Relationship: Over 4 years
Marital Status: Single
Height: 5'6"
Body Type: Average
Hair Color: Black
Religion: Baptist
Ethnicity: Black
Your Profession: yes (there's an intelligent answer . . . not)
Your Income Level: Less than $25,000 (the understatement of the year)
Education: High school (I still don't buy it)
Your parents had: 3 children (one of whom is dumber than a bag of rocks)
Eye color: Blue
Would you date someone who has BBW or a few extra body pounds selected as a body type? Yes
Do you smoke? Occasionally

Would you date someone who smokes? Yes

Do you do drugs? No

Do you drink? Socially

Do you own a car? Yes

Do you have children? Yes

Do you want children? Want children

Would you date someone who has kids? Yes

Do you have pets? No pets

Your birth order: Second born

How ambitious are you? Very ambitious

Headline: very love able

Description: Likes to have fun a lot

I also don't buy the line about him not doing drugs. No one in his right mind could possibly be this dumb.

For good measure, hours after creating his profile there, he tried again at WellHello for the seventh time.

Saturday, November 9

When the sun goes down, David Coleman comes out to play.

Overnight, he signed up for two more dating sites. The first was EbonyFlirt, where they say he could meet naughty black singles in no time. That is assuming you actually sign up with your own email address. Like most of the others, they didn't wait for the email verification before spamming away. What a shame that he missed that new private message from Simone. Once again I logged in, like I did with Plenty of Fish, changed the email to point to his Yahoo account and set his status to "I am the dumbest man alive because I keep signing up to these sites using someone else's email address."

I tried to do the same with the next site he signed me up for. A site where you can flirt and set up dates with ebony cuties like Candace892, who sent him a "frisky" message. But the status message wasn't approved. I was tempted to send a message to the site admins asking why it was rejected. After all, it is true. Coleman is the dumbest human on the planet. At least the dumbest human who isn't locked up in a high-security mental institution.

Later in the morning, he signed up for two more dating sites three minutes apart. Sadly, in each case, the same status message I tried to leave wasn't approved. Go figure.

Amid all the activity on the online dating front over the last week, I had completely forgotten about Nintendo. That is, until two more verification attempts landed in my inbox later in the day, bringing the total number to 40.

I feel like sending him a card to mark the occasion.

Sunday, November 10

Today, I went more on the offensive with David Coleman.

Using an anonymous email service that uses disposable addresses, I sent this message to his Yahoo account:

Attention David Coleman

Dear Mr. Coleman:

Are you are aware that the emails for all the sites you've been signing up for over the past three months are in fact going to SOMEONE ELSE?? Yes, you have been signing someone else up for everything including Snapchat, Larters Bank, Varo and all the filthy adult dating sites you're trying to find solace in. Not to mention your communications from Roberta Sedaris at the motorcycle school and Sandra Harrison at Southeastern Interstate University. Did I mention your rejections from Bank of America, Discover Student Loans, etc., etc.? And the many verification attempts with Nintendo?

Has it dawned on you that after all this time, you've been using SOMEONE ELSE's account instead of your own? The world is not out to get you, Mr. Coleman. You and you alone are at fault. Ask one of your four children for help. Or even your ex-wife LaToya.

In the email, I made a point to use the actual names of people he's been trying to communicate with. Even his ex-wife's name. I wanted to send a shiver down his spine. Something to get his attention. Maybe then he'll wake up and stop using my email address.

But if he got the message, it didn't sink in. Because late in the day, he signed me up for another dating site, the self-proclaimed #1 transgender community on the net. So he's really branching out now. Probably because he's been striking out everywhere else. So this time, I sent him a few texts, again using that same anonymous email service.

Hey asshole, ever wonder why you're not getting any responses from all these sites you're signing up to?
Maybe it's because you're entering SOMEONE ELSE'S EMAIL ADDRESS!!!!
Like you did with TS Scene last night.
How many more sites are you going to sign up for before you realize that you're using the WRONG EMAIL ADDRESS?
This is the classic definition of insanity – doing the same thing over and over again and expecting a different result.

Monday, November 11

With no activity overnight, I had started thinking David Coleman might have gotten the message.

That is, until I got a verification request from Stripchat, a site with free live sex cams and adult chat with naked girls. At least they were good enough to insist on verification before filling my inbox. They also sent me a system-generated password that Coleman can't possibly guess.

So I went on the offensive again.

For starters, using his mobile number, I signed up for alerts at a dozen different places. Fight fire with fire. I followed that up by sending him the following texts:

HEY COLEMAN, YOU MUST BE THE DUMBEST MAN ON THE FACE OF THE EARTH.
USE YOUR OWN EMAIL ADDRESS FOR A CHANGE!
YOUR SON JAMARCUS PROBABLY HAS MORE BRAINS THAN YOU DO.

Finally, I tried creating a Nintendo account with his Yahoo address and spammed him with about a dozen verification attempts. See how he likes it. And maybe it will show him that Nintendo verifications really do work . . . when you use your own email address instead of someone else's.

What else can I do?

Wednesday, November 13

Just when I thought I might have finally gotten through to David Coleman, he's back at it again.

Following a day off from having to sanitize my inbox, he signed up for five more dating sites overnight. Three of them, in fact, came within a half hour of each other. As I went through changing passwords and turning off the email alerts, I learned that he has had less than 10 sex partners, he feels blonde is the sexiest hair color and he rates himself a two on a scale of one to 10 as a lover. Maybe that's why LaToya left him. Or more likely because the man's a complete idiot.

So to follow up, I sent a few texts his way. Not that I really expect any of them to register with him. More just for myself. I needed to vent.

COLEMAN, YOU REALLY ARE A DUMBASS.
WHEN WILL YOU FIGURE OUT THAT YOU'RE SIGNING UP TO ALL THESE FILTHY SITES WITH SOMEONE ELSE'S EMAIL ADDRESS???

And again a few hours later.

HEY COLEMAN, YOU WANT TO KNOW WHAT THE DEFINITION OF INSANITY IS?
THAT'S WHEN YOU KEEP SIGNING UP FOR DATING WEBSITES WITH SOMEONE ELSE'S EMAIL ADDRESS OVER AND OVER AGAIN AND STILL EXPECT TO GET A RESPONSE.

Thursday, November 14

Today I got confirmation that David Coleman didn't pursue the motorcycle course.

From: Roberta Sedaris
Subject: Still interested?
To: David Coleman

Hello,

I want to take the time to thank you for the chance to conduct the interview with you. I have not heard from you since the interview so I wanted to reach out.

Based on my notes from the interview conducted, your goals align with what we offer here at Central Florida Motorcycle Institute. I would like to recommend you to our programs and I want to ensure you have the opportunity to reserve your spot.

This might not be the right time for you to continue your education. If that is the case, I can certainly understand. What is important is that you find something that interests you. If this is the case, maybe someone you know who may have an interest in one of our programs feel free to pass on my information.

Keep in mind that new classes start every few weeks. Therefore, when you are ready, please let me know how I can help you. With your permission, I would like to continue to follow up with you.

I look forward to talking with you again in the near future.

Thanks,

Roberta Sedaris
Admissions Representative
Central Florida Motorcycle Institute
For Students. For Industry. For Success.

Confidential

This e-mail and any files transmitted with it are the property of the Central Florida Motorcycle Institute and/or its affiliates, are confidential, and are intended solely for the use of the individual or entity to whom this e-mail is addressed. If you are not one of the named recipients or otherwise have reason to believe that you have received this e-mail in error, please notify the sender and delete this message immediately from your computer. Any other use, retention, dissemination, forwarding, printing or copying of this e-mail is strictly prohibited.

Perhaps it all fell apart because he couldn't put his stuff in storage. That and the failure to correctly answer the first question of the enrollment process – what's your email address?

I got a particularly good laugh out of the disclaimer at the end. I don't owe her or Coleman a damned thing. When she and Coleman keep shoving this stuff in my inbox, it's mine, plain and simple.

Friday, November 15

After more than 48 hours of inactivity, David Coleman went on another rampage.

Early in the morning, he signed up for a second time at EbonyFlirt. The first time, I deleted the account, but this time, I just changed the password and turned off all the email notifications.

Then I sent this off to him:

JESUS CHRIST COLEMAN, HAVEN'T YOU FIGURED IT OUT YET WHY YOU'RE NOT GETTING ANY RESPONSES TO EBONYFLIRT AND ALL THOSE DATING WEBSITES???
IT'S BECAUSE YOU'RE USING SOMEONE ELSE'S EMAIL ADDRESS!!!!

Unfazed, a couple of hours later, Coleman tried to sign up with Varo for the ninth time. Which prompted a couple more angry texts from me.

HEY COLEMAN, JUST GOT YOUR VARO VERIFICATION CODE. YOU KNOW YOU MIGHT FIND IT HELPFUL IF YOU HAD IT SENT TO YOUR OWN EMAIL ADDRESS INSTEAD!

Using the same anonymous email service, I also sent this off to Varo's support address:

Hello, I am the legitimate owner of david82@FreeAMail.net, the email address a David Coleman of Deland, Florida is attempting to create a profile with.

Please inform Mr. Coleman that he is again using someone else's email address, and if you could, block this address from further verification attempts. I have never attempted to do business with Varo and don't foresee such a need in future.

Thank you.

Maybe they can get through to him. Because I sure can't.

Moving on, he signed up for a guide at Unemployment Claims. So he's still unemployed. Hardly a surprise. So I sent him a couple of more texts:

HEY COLEMAN, GOT YOUR UNEMPLOYMENT CLAIM REQUEST.

NO WONDER YOU CAN'T FIND WORK, BECAUSE YOU'RE SO STUPID AS TO KEEP GIVING OUT SOMEONE ELSE'S EMAIL ADDRESS INSTEAD OF YOUR OWN.

But if he's indeed getting this stuff and reading it, it still isn't getting through, as evidenced by his most recent handiwork later in the evening.

From: ClassesUSA
Subject: David, We've Received Your Inquiry
To: David Coleman
Hello David,

Congratulations on getting matched! Your recent request for information has been processed.

You'd be a good fit for:

School: Parker University Global
School: Southeastern Interstate University

Here's what'll happen next:
You'll be contacted shortly by a highly recognized college or education provider listed above to discuss your career and education goals. You'll be provided with important information, and any questions you have about obtaining your degree can be answered.

All of us at classesUSA greatly appreciate you letting us be a part of your education.

Warmest Regards,
The classesUSA Team

This guy is so stupid he wouldn't be a good fit for Romper Room. But they'd probably still take him anyway if he had the money. Except that he doesn't have much of that either. Poor guy.

Saturday, November 16

David Coleman signed up with two more dating sites overnight.

I'm shocked . . . NOT!

The first was OneBBW. BBW dating for big beautiful women and guys who love them, they say. Except that this guy can't love them because they sent me the system-generated password to access the account instead of him. Sticking with the BBW theme, next was FindBBWSex. Too bad he missed out on a private message from olajuwonerlan49. And another message saying that if he upgraded his account, he could initiate dating with Abisola.

I knew it wouldn't do any good, but I still had to send Coleman another couple of texts.

Hey Coleman, you sure seem to like those online dating sites. BBW seems to be a fetish of yours.
But don't you think you might get more action if you actually used YOUR OWN EMAIL ADDRESS instead of someone else's????

Next, I sent this off to Roberta Sedaris. Just like with Varo, maybe she can get through to him when they talk on the phone.

Roberta,

I am the legitimate owner of the email address david82@FreeAMail.net, the one you have been using in your attempt to electronically correspond with David Coleman. I am not David Coleman and thus, please do not forward any more communication intended for him to that address.

If you will be speaking with him on the phone, please try to impress upon Mr. Coleman that he is continuing to mistakenly give out my email address as his own, which is why he has not received any of your emails.

Thank you.

Meanwhile, Coleman remains a busy little beaver online. For starters, he signed up with Happy Home Insider. It's nice that he wants to learn how to be a better homeowner. Sometimes it can be hard work. But it's hard to get info to your inbox when you don't give them your own email address. Then he signed up for a Reinvent Your Life Summit. On November 21, the speaker is going to share a secret that took him from dead broke to $5 million in under two years and gave him back control of his time and his life. It will be a fun and interactive experience, he says. Explore his unconventional approach to investing. VIP attendees to this online event can send him video questions on trading, the markets or anything else. Nothing is off limits. Including insider trading, as a subsequent email would reveal.

Soon after reading this, I got a notification that Coleman is pursuing another school.

From: Jeff Garson
Subject: PARKER GLOBAL ADMISSIONS PROCESS
To: David Coleman

Dear Future Parker University Global Student,

It was a pleasure speaking with you today regarding your educational goals. Please complete the following steps to begin the process of enrollment:

STEP ONE: Free Application for Federal Student Aid (FAFSA)

· Access the FAFSA
· Enter school code for Parker University Global
· Submit FAFSA application
· Please forward confirmation email to me

STEP TWO: Parker University Global Admissions Application

· You will receive an email to complete your online application
· Create a password
· Fill out application
· You MUST electronically sign the enrollment agreement

STEP THREE: Master Promissory Note Instructions

· Select the Loan Master Promissory Note Log In
· Select Parker University Global as school name
· Please forward confirmation email to me

STEP FOUR: ENTRANCE COUNSELING

· Select the Log In
· Please forward confirmation email to me

Congratulations! You are on your way!

Jeff Garson
Admissions Advisor

So I sent this off to Jeff Garson. It's all I can do at this point.

Mr. Garson, it is my understanding you were speaking with David Coleman of Deland, Florida this morning and that he has mistakenly given you my email address (david82@FreeAMail.net) as his. Please do not forward any further communication intended for Mr. Coleman to me.

If you speak to him again, please try to impress upon Mr. Coleman that my email address is not his and ask him to provide you with his correct email address.

Thank you.

Later in the afternoon, I got an email from another admissions advisor at SIU. I guess they're still interested in having him, or Daffy Duck, as a student. I suppose they don't particularly care either way just as long as Daffy can pay the tuition.

Before winding up an exhausting day for both of us, he signed me up for two more dating sites two minutes apart.

I keep wondering how stupid he can possibly be.

But sadly, Coleman is taking that as a challenge.

Saturday, November 23

It had been nearly a full week since anything from David Coleman had popped up in my inbox.

But just when I started thinking that maybe Jeff Garson or Roberta Sedaris might have been able to get through to him, he signed up at Uberhorny and AmazingFlings early in the morning. Later in the day, he tried twice more at WellHello (for those keeping score, that makes nine such attempts) and tried again at OneNightFriend, one of the sites he had tried a couple of weeks earlier. And after I had changed the email address in the verification popup, he went and created another profile there using my address less than an hour later. Which resulted in a ton of spam even before I got the verification request. Do I know Autumn? A juicy girl, Adrianne, a 24-year-old from "Fort Lauderal" is looking for a man. There's a new message from Ericka2! Shadow10 passionately awaits you! Or I could upgrade my membership to dating with Arreona. Once again, I changed the address in the verification popup. Let someone else deal with this shit.

Sadly, Coleman wasn't done for the night as he signed me up for two more dating sites. I soon got a new message from Karol62. A yummy girl, Julie from Hialeah, just viewed his profile. Where have you been so long, she asks? Pretty locals are aspiring to flirt with you. Have an affair with your match!

The week-long break couldn't have been an accident. Coleman probably was speaking with Jeff and/or Roberta and got spooked. Maybe he thinks he's been hacked and that by lying low for a while, the "hacker" would leave him alone.

That guy is a special kind of stupid.

Monday, November 25

David Coleman is running low on dating sites.

So now he's busy going back to the ones he signed me up with before hoping they'll work now.

He started by trying ComeWithYou again. Your fun dating, hookup and swingers site with style, they say. Then he tried it again three hours later, prompting another couple of texts from me.

> *Hey Coleman, sorry to hear that your love life is in the crapper.*
> *ComeWithYou might offer some solace, but if you want to get into these filthy dating sites, it might help if you entered your OWN EMAIL ADDRESS!!!!*

Wednesday, November 27

If at first you don't succeed, try, try again.

Today, David Coleman tried again at WellHello. That's 10 such attempts with them.

Yesterday, he tried Uberhorny again. He's only tried there twice.

Thursday, November 28

I'm finding it amazing how David Coleman can even keep track of all the sites he's signed me up for.

Overnight, he tried to get back in at BBWDesire, a site where I had changed the password. He actually used the link to try to retrieve his login credentials, but of course, the email came to me and not to him.

A few hours later, he actually found a new site to sign up for, forcing me to go in and lock him out. Poor sucker missed out on a private message from Chelcie171. And possible love from Nax476 from Hollywood, a "yummy girl" who viewed his profile. He also missed out on the chance to upgrade his membership to initiate dating with BlowinJOB69.

Saturday, November 30

After a couple of days off for the Thanksgiving holiday, David Coleman is back in action.

Going back in the archives, he made another attempt at MaturesForFuck. The site's name is an oxymoron if I've ever seen one. Then again, Coleman himself is an oxymoron. Not in the literal sense, but as a cross between an ox and a moron. Stubborn and stupid.

Sunday, December 1

David Coleman found four new dating sites to sign up for today.

One of them was IamNaughty.

He'd have had more luck with IamStupid.

Monday, December 2

David Coleman tried only one dating site today.

It was an old one where I just deactivated the profile but didn't change the password. This time I went back in and did it right, locking him out completely. What a shame, because he's missing out on new friends like xxhoney44xx, flawedbabe, nerdyblackbae and zoaondi991. But I'm sure that won't stop him. He's already found so many of those sites and I'm sure there's more just around the corner that he can't wait to sign me up for.

Tuesday, December 3

Another day, another new dating site for David Coleman.

And me.

Niki had apparently shown interest in Coleman's profile before I deleted the account.

Interestingly, he used 1982dodge as his password instead of 1982Dodge. Perhaps he figured the upper case "D" was the problem. In his profile, he listed his occupation as "landscape." In other words, if, in fact, it's true that he has an occupation, he mows lawns.

Later in the day, he tried again at WellHello. That makes 11 such attempts.

Those blades of grass he's cutting are more intelligent than he is.

Thursday, December 5

After a day off, David Coleman is back in the saddle.

In the morning, he signed up at one new dating site and another he tried for the second time. Too bad that Coleman missed out on a girl with a naughty pic who browsed him as well as private messages from yoko589 and Shae. Corine9696 liked him and sayhith41 added him to her favorites.

But it wasn't just all fun and games with him today.

He signed up for a quit smoking group with Tobacco Free Florida, which will meet at 2:00 pm on January 7 at a hospital in Miami.

So again, to humor myself, I sent him a couple more nasty texts:

Hey Coleman, great to hear that you've signed up to try to quit smoking.
Maybe you should have signed up for a brain transplant while you're at it, because you
still keep giving out an email address that DOESN'T BELONG TO YOU!!!!!!!

Unfazed, Coleman marched on. Later in the evening, Katherine Rydman at Florida Career College sent me an email asking Coleman to call her in response to a previous inquiry. So I responded as follows:

Katherine, I am the legitimate owner of david82@FreeAMail.net, the address you were trying to reach David Coleman at. As it is not his email address, please do not send any more communication intended for Mr. Coleman to that address.

If you will be speaking with him in future, please ask him to provide you with his correct email address and, if you could, please try to impress upon Mr. Coleman that he continues to give out the wrong email address to others, including you.

Who knows, if she talks to him, maybe it will buy me a few days of freedom. That's all I can realistically hope for at this point.

Before the end of the day, he found another new dating site, where Anna wanted to chat with him. I rerouted the account to point to his Yahoo address. Maybe the two of them can hook up there.

Friday, December 6

David Coleman took a walk on the wild side overnight.

This time, he signed up with a new dating site that touts itself as the #1 bisexual dating site for bi singles and couples. Our site is designed for bisexual, bi-curious individuals and bi couples, they say. Here you can find other sexy and open-minded singles and couples who are looking to explore their sexuality, chat, hook up and more. Maybe he wants to get adventurous. Or more likely, he's just desperate, since he's been running low on inventory for new sites to sign up for.

Monday, December 9

Following a weekend off, David Coleman tried an old favorite again.

He made yet another attempt at WellHello. That brings the total number to 12.

There must be some particularly hot babes on that site whom he wants to hook up with.

But he'll never find out for sure until he starts using his own email address instead of mine.

Tuesday, December 10

Warding off David Coleman's online activity is consuming way too much of my time.

Just before the noon hour, he signed me up at another new dating site called MyPrivateFling. Obviously it's not that private, at least for him, since he keeps wanting to share those flings with me. Thankfully, they're one of the few places that insist on activation before he can get anywhere. But obviously he still hasn't gotten the message. So I sent him some more texts. What the hell.

Hey Coleman, just got your activation email for MyPrivateFling.
Want to know why it came to me instead of you?
That's because YOU DIDN'T USE YOUR OWN EMAIL ADDRESS, YOU
DUMBASS!!!!!

Later in the day, I got this from Parker University Global:

From: Marlene Finley
Subject: New Year's Registration Has Started-Parker University Global
To: David Coleman

Hello there,

Happy Tuesday,Hope all is well. Winter New Year Registration starts now. I'm a Senior Advisor here at Parker Global, following up with you about your enrollment process. Your advisor shared with me that your ready to move forward to complete your enrollment for January 8th Start Date. However we have a few last steps. We received a school application for you,your file is pending. Below are the instructions to complete the steps, if you have already completed the fafsa please let me know. I can assist with these documents, let's work on completing your enrollment so that you can enjoy your Holiday Break and be ready for the New Year. After the holidays we can choose your live seminar classes and orientation schedule times. Let me know if you have any other questions in regards to this process. Please email me back what time tomorrow we can give you a call.

I'm looking forward to a great school year.
talk to you soon;

Mrs. Marlene Finley
Admissions Advisor

Obviously my email didn't get through to either Coleman or them. So I tried again.

Mrs. Finley, I am the legitimate owner of david82@FreeAMail.net, the address you sent an email to intended for David Coleman. As I previously requested of one of your colleagues, please do not send any more communication to that address, as it does not belong to Mr. Coleman.

If you wish to contact Mr. Coleman in regard to his enrollment, I encourage you to call him. Please try to impress upon him that he continues to quote someone else's email address and ask him to provide you with his correct email address.

Thank you.

Then he signed me up at TextNow, a service you can use to call and text anywhere in North America for free. Thankfully, they offered an "Unauthorize Email" link in their verification email, much like Snapchat, so I used it. See how many times he tries to get it back.

Wednesday, December 11

David Coleman was playing games overnight.

At 2:00 am, I got an email from Coin Master, telling me I've got access to my very own Balloon Frenzy. Apparently it's some kind of Facebook game. At least I was able to unsubscribe.

At least that was all.

Maybe Marlene Finley got a hold of him and it's starting to sink in that he's been using someone else's email address.

Keeping my fingers crossed.

Monday, December 16

It was a nice break, but as they say, all good things must come to an end.

Early in the morning, David Coleman requested more information from Kilton University.

From: Kilton University
Subject: Thank you for your interest in Kilton University

To: David Coleman

Dear David,
Thank you for your interest in Kilton University.

We have received your request for information. We will be in contact with you to see how we may assist you in achieving your education and career goals.

Kilton University
Admissions Department

Followed soon thereafter by this:

From: Michael Nelson
Subject: Your New Journey
To: David Coleman

Dear David Coleman

It was wonderful speaking with you earlier today and I look forward to helping you get started in BA-Business Administration-Management. It is an exciting time and one that will open new opportunities for you. I look forward to seeing you at our scheduled appointment.

Sincerely,

Michael Nelson
Admissions Counselor
Kilton University

So I sent this off to Michael. Maybe it will buy me another few days of peace. Or not.

Michael, I am the legitimate owner of david82@FreeAMail.net, the address David Coleman has quoted you as being his. Please do not send any more communication to that address as it belongs to me and not to Mr. Coleman.

When speaking with him, please try to impress upon Mr. Coleman that he continues time and again to quote someone else's email address and ask him to provide you with his correct email address.

Thank you.

I couldn't help but laugh when I read that Coleman was interested in a Business Administration – Management program. This is a guy who can't even figure out his own email address, and he's going to run a business? I don't think so. In any event, it would be funny to be a fly on the wall for that meeting.

I found it interesting that this was the second time he's tried Kilton. Perhaps he's pissed at the other colleges because they won't email him at "his" address, so he's making the rounds in the hopes of finding one that will.

For the record, it has now been four months since the name David Coleman first fouled my inbox.

Wednesday, December 18

This morning, I got this from Kilton University:

From: KILTON UNIVERSITY
Subject: An important message from KILTON UNIVERSITY
To: David Coleman

Dear David,

We have attempted to reach you several times via phone regarding your interest in Kilton University.

It's not too late! We are actively enrolling for our upcoming start!

Please contact us by phone to speak with a helpful admissions counselor.

Thank you for your interest!

Kilton University
Admissions Department

Hmmm. I guess that meeting didn't go too well. Maybe he got pissed off when Michael had the gall to suggest he was using someone else's email address.

After the Holidays

Saturday, December 28

David Coleman must have been too busy over the holidays to go online.

But sadly, he's back.

Overnight, he signed up at SugarBBW. Find your big beauty here, they say. Janil5678 from El Portal viewed his profile, Kionna really likes him and he has a new private message from maribelle_08. Ramona, 54, from Miami also wants to tell him something. I'd like to tell him something too. So I did.

> *Hey Coleman, got your emails for SugarBBW.*
> *Start using your own email address, you retard!!!!*

Interestingly, he used a different password this time. Maybe he really does think he's been hacked. But if he thinks "his" account has been compromised, why does he keep using it? It's not going to be any less compromised if you lay off it for several days.

Sunday, December 29

David Coleman is getting back into the swing of things.

Overnight, he signed up at another new dating site. The 29-year-old "bighotfuckbud" said, "Hello david8258, I was taught not to speak to strangers, so tell me something about yourself..x.x." Then there was this message from 44-year-old "xxunperfectxx":

> *Hello david8258, Your special friend xxunperfectxx has a new pending chat message for you. She is available now for a private chat and wants you to reply soon.*

After making his 13th attempt at WellHello, he tried two more new dating sites. He missed private messages from Sherilee4 and Katlynn and will never know that Carmalita passionately awaits him.

Interestingly, he went back to his usual password once again. The one he used the previous night was probably just an accident. He didn't get a brain wave. He's just stupid.

Monday, December 30

In a shocking development (NOT!), there was more overnight activity from David Coleman.

After signing me up at InstantHookups, he turned his attention across the ocean and signed me up for a couple of sites featuring Russian and Ukrainian mail-order brides. He is getting desperate. More for a brain than for online companionship.

Later in the day, he found another new dating site to sign me up for. It was the 70th different dating site since this sordid affair began more than four months ago.

And yet he seems no closer to figuring it out.

I'm at a loss for words. How someone this stupid can function in society is beyond me.

Tuesday, December 31

David Coleman had to get in one more dating site before the year was out.

And soon after came a private message from chubbiplay.

Too bad he'll never see it.

Wednesday, January 1

The new year brought more good tidings from David Coleman.

Overnight, he tried three more dating sites, one new and two old, flooding my inbox with more spam. Everyone from AmySullivan, 29, of Hialeah Gardens to tellmeiamhot69, 31, of Miami to RideMeCowboy, 31, of Carol City to HollyHeavenly, 35, of Miami wants to get to know him. If they only knew. On one of his profiles, he said he's looking for females aged 18-26 and he "likes sex all day long and fun."

Near the middle of the day, he turned his attention away from the dating sites long enough to sign me up at a new online bank called Fold, based out of Bangalore. His spot on the waiting list would move up for each person he invites, but that would require him giving his own email address, not just one he pulled out of his ass. So he won't get that opportunity, as I promptly unsubscribed him and took him off the list. The fact that he's still pursuing these obscure banks, however, is another indicator that his credit is still in the crapper. For the life of me, I can't figure out why.

Late in the day, he signed me up for two more dating sites 10 minutes apart. Extricating myself from those two proved particularly difficult. The former insisted on knowing why I was deleting the profile, so I said, "Consider being less sleazy by insisting on email verification first." They followed that with an email with the subject "Please accept our apologies." Not for spamming me without verifying the email. But because their servers were overloaded and he was unable to log in. So they're offering a discount on paid membership. As they say in Texas, El Paso. The latter would only "suspend" the profile and wouldn't do a full delete until I uploaded government-issued photo ID. I'll be sure to get on that right away. Or not.

Friday, January 3

After a day off, there was more overnight activity from David Coleman.

He tried two more times to get on WellHello. The tally for Nintendo 2.0 now stands at 15.

Mixed in between was a new site called SimpleFlirts. Amazingly, they actually insisted on confirming the email before spamming me. They wouldn't even let him into his profile without email confirmation.

If only the rest of those sites operated the same way.

Later in the morning, he signed up for another new dating site that didn't have the same scruples as SimpleFlirts does. So after extricating myself from their clutches, I sent Coleman a few more texts. Again, more to vent.

Coleman, you retard!
Got your confirmation email for meetmilfy.
Start using your own email address, you asshole!

Back at the ranch, later in the day, he must have made another inquiry with the motorcycle school.

From: Steven Bedson
Subject: Here is your CFMI ViewBook
To: David Coleman

Hi, David Coleman

Central Florida Motorcycle Institute (CFMI) is leading the way to meet the growing demand for professional, entry-level motorcycle technicians.

If you would like to learn more about our programs, click here to view the Online Program Brochure.

Feel free to contact me with any questions, and I'll be in touch soon!

Steven Bedson
Admissions Representative

So since they didn't get the message the first time, I tried again.

Steven, I am the legitimate owner of david82@FreeAMail.net, the email address you were trying to reach David Coleman at. As it is not Mr. Coleman's email address and having already noted that to your colleague Roberta Sedaris, please do not send any more communication to that address.

If you will be speaking with him at any point in the future, please try to impress upon Mr. Coleman that he continues to quote someone else's email address as his own and ask him to provide you with his correct email address.

Thank you.

Saturday, January 4

David Coleman went on another rampage today.

His first target was Dating Egg. Not once, but twice. Enter your email address to start chatting, they say. No credit card required. Yet. But at least they insist on email verification before allowing you to create an account.

Not so with the next two, however. The latter called itself the best international dating site for singles over 40. He's still a few years away from 40, but what's age but a number? In both cases, I logged in using his usual password, changed the password and turned off the email alerts before finally deactivating the profile. They wouldn't delete the account without contacting support. If only they would make you jump through the same hoops to create an account in the first place.

A half hour later, he signed me up at Fuckbook using the user ID 28divad. That's david82 spelled backwards. Pretty creative for someone otherwise so stupid. But to their credit, Fuckbook is another of the good guys and won't spam you until you confirm your email address. Unlike Larters Bank, among many others.

Sunday, January 5

Still oblivious to his own stupidity, David Coleman signed up for three more dating sites overnight.

And because he used my email address again, he missed out on messages from Juggalhippie and wetwetx92. What a shame. At one of the sites, he took the time to upload a new selfie behind his house with his garbage cans and two cars in the background. So I grabbed the shot, created a meme with it using the caption "I'm the dumbest human alive because I don't even know my own email address" and sent it to him. As a good friend said to me, if that doesn't get his attention, nothing will.

For good measure, Coleman also tried to get on WellHello for the 16th time.

Monday, January 6

Kilton University is getting as bad as those dating sites.

From: Angela Bishop
Subject: Career Advancement
To: David Coleman

Good Day David

Trust that you are having a great day orientation starts this Wednesday January 8.

Reply so I may assist you with transitioning to your new Career Advancement.

Kind Regards

Angela Bishop
Admission Counselor
Kilton University

So I sent this in reply:

Angela, I am the legitimate owner of david82@FreeAMail.net. Sadly, Kilton University remains committed to trying to contact David Coleman at this address despite a previous email to one of your colleagues alerting him that this address does not belong to Mr. Coleman.

Will you please make a note in Mr. Coleman's file that david82@FreeAMail.net is not his email address and STOP sending emails to that address.

Thank you.

It should be noted that after Coleman had been so active over the last few days, I didn't hear a thing from him all day. Perhaps that meme did have some effect. He must be scratching his head wondering how this stranger got his picture.

Tuesday, January 7

David Coleman might be spooked.

But he's determined not to let that "hacker" stop him.

Late in the afternoon, he signed me up at SnapSext, a site where you can trade naked selfies. Interestingly, when I went in to delete the account, I noticed that he didn't upload a selfie this time. He's probably still freaked out about having his picture in the hands of a stranger, yet he continues to use that stranger's email address when signing up for websites.

Stupid is as stupid does.

Thursday, January 9

After a bit of a lull, David Coleman is back at it again.

Bright and early, he gave WellHello another shot, his 17th such attempt. This was soon followed by a new signup at MyHornySingles.

So I fired off a few more texts.

Hey Coleman, got another verification for WellHello.
Want to know why it's coming to me instead of you?
That's because you're not using your own email address.
Let me spell this out for you clearly.
DAVID82 -at- FREEAMAIL.NET DOESN'T BELONG TO YOU!!!!
I demand you STOP harassing me at once!
Start using your own account to sign up for all your filthy websites!

Unfazed, he made another attempt at OneNightFriend a few hours later.

To say the least, he's a pretty slow learner.

Friday, January 10

This time, David Coleman signed up for a newsletter from an adult shop.

Perhaps he's getting prepared for when he meets one of these online hotties in person.

Which he could probably arrange if only he would use his own email address.

Saturday, January 11

David Coleman tried WellHello again.

For those keeping score, that's the 18th time.

For the life of me, I can't figure out what makes that site so special.

But then again, I'm not David Coleman.

I actually have a brain.

Monday, January 13

More overnight activity from David Coleman.

He tried again at HelloHotties. Meet a hottie and get naughty, they say. And he tried one more time at OneNightFriend. Honestly, the guy is like an alcoholic. He just can't help himself. Even when he gets spooked, like with the picture or when he hears from third parties I've contacted, he stays away from the bottle for a few days, then falls off the wagon again. I'm also surprised through all of this that I haven't received any communication from his friends or family. After all, it's not like he's shy about spreading his (my) email address around.

So I decided to send him a couple of more memes. The first featured the Philosoraptor with the caption "I created another account using someone else's email address, and I still can't figure out why I never get the activation emails." Next, I used one of his old selfies with the caption "When the owner of david82@FreeAMail.net asks how stupid can you be, I take it as a challenge."

Give him something to stew on for a while.

Tuesday, January 14

All David Coleman seems to be stewing on is why he can't get on WellHello.

He tried again overnight and once more late in the day.

That makes 20 such attempts.

In between, he signed up at flirtmoms. The greatest single moms dating site, they say. Be brave enough to be happy again!

He (I) also got a message from another old site he signed me up with:

Hey it's Alexis ... Do you want me to send you my new pics?
Send me a text on my mobile (724) 555-6031 ... ttys

Sorry, Alexis, I'll pass on that.

Wednesday, January 15

David Coleman signed up for another dating site overnight.

Find attached, single or adventurous people near you, they say.

But he didn't try WellHello again. So I sent a few texts his way. Just to have a little fun with him.

Hey Coleman, planning to sign up at WellHello again tonight?
Let me save you the trouble . . . if you use david82 -at- FreeAMail.net, it's not going to work.
Just like it hasn't worked for the 20 times you've already tried it.
But if you use your own email address, I guarantee you it will work.
Think about it.

Thursday, January 16

Stop the presses.

David Coleman didn't sign up for a dating site overnight.

I wonder if he's OK.

More likely, he's just spooked. Probably sitting in his hovel wondering what's going on. But he'll fall off the wagon again. It's just a matter of time. He hasn't figured it out and at this point, I doubt if he ever will.

One has to wonder if his mother drank heavily or used drugs when she was pregnant with him.

Friday, January 17

Rumors of David Coleman's death have been greatly exaggerated.

Two more attempts at WellHello brought the tally to 22.

In between, he tried tendermeets. Join and let love happen to you, they say. Or to someone else when you give their address instead of your own.

Sunday, January 19

Never one to stay on the wagon too long, David Coleman signed me up for another dating site. You can easily find the profile of your dreams by using our advanced search tools, they say. And they offer a secure environment for members to flirt online.

Members who give their own email addresses instead of someone else's.

Monday, January 20

Another day, another nocturnal dating site signup for David Coleman.

This time, he tried again at Fuckbook. Except that this time, he used the user ID 28divad66. The last time he tried that site, he just used 28divad. Perhaps he thinks that by adding the 66, that's going to make all the difference (see Nintendo). Or more likely, because they wouldn't let him use the same user ID he tried the first time since it's still on their files even though I never confirmed the email address.

Tuesday, January 21

Just when I had begun to think that David Coleman was losing his will to carry on the battle, he gets a second wind.

Or in this case, a hundredth wind.

Near the middle of the day, he signed up with NearbyFlings, and six minutes later, he tried DateYou. A half hour later, he tried WellHello for the 23rd time and then tried again at Flirt.com.

So, to humor myself, I sent him some more texts. What the hell.

Hey Coleman, still haven't figured it out yet, have you?
It doesn't matter how many times you try to sign up with dating sites using david82 -at-FreeAMail.net.
It's not going to work.
That's because that address doesn't belong to you!

Minutes later, almost as if to show me who's boss, the 23 previous attempts be damned, he tried for the 24th time at WellHello. He must figure that one of these days, it's bound to work. He just needs to stick with it.

In the evening, he created a new account at DateYou, replacing the one I had rerouted to his Yahoo account, then he tried again with two more dating sites before trying WellHello one more time.

Friday, January 24

If only David Coleman knew that someone wanted to hire him.

Following up on Coleman's application back in October, a recruiter sent a bulk mailing to him and hundreds of others. How courteous of her to reveal the email addresses of each and every applicant.

From: Lori Green

Subject: CBX Expedited: Sponsorship & Job Offer (CDL Class-A)

To: David Coleman + 253 others

Hello!

YOUR SKILLS ARE NEEDED!

CBX is expanding our Fleet size and we need DRIVERS who are interested in establishing a promising career with us!

This is Lori from CBX; one of the Job-Sponsorship Recruiters. We are going through rapid growth. It's been an amazing quarter for us and we need company Drivers who are team-players, disciplined and career-oriented. The sooner I have a complete application sent back, the sooner I'll be able to review your options with us and get you scheduled for work/training with us.

If you're interested in this opportunity; kindly use the below link to apply with a complete application. I will follow up with you to go over the application and discuss the next steps. It would be best to use a computer to fill out the application. Phones will encounter an error.

I can assure you (this is not one of those Nigerian scam emails)! I have had a few people who were sceptical.

I will reach out to you once this is returned to me. Attached in the information packet for your perusal.

Respectfully,

Lori Green

Driver Recruiter

So I replied as follows:

Lori, I am the legitimate owner of david82@FreeAMail.net, the address David Coleman mistakenly gave your company as his. Please remove that address from your files and do not send any more communication to that address.

If you wish to reach out to Mr. Coleman, I urge you to contact him by phone at 786-555-7546. In that conversation, please try to impress upon Mr. Coleman that he continues to quote someone else's email address as his own.

Furthermore, I urge you to be much more careful when sending out mass mailings such as these as, in this case, you revealed more than 250 emails of prospective applicants.

Thank you.

That evening, Coleman signed me up for the third time at DateYou, forcing me to go in and delete the account. Again.

Tuesday, January 28

Three days of peace ended when David Coleman tried MyHornySingles and DateYou again yesterday evening.

So this morning, I decided to jerk his chain a little. Using a free email account with the name "isabellapsn," a girl who had liked his profile on one of the dating sites he signed me up with, I sent the following texts:

Hello dave8225, Going to keep perving on pics or tell me something about you?
Hello dave8225, Don't be shy. Love to hear from you.

Sure enough, Coleman took the bait.

Hello
how are you
not shy

Not only did I get him going, but it confirmed that I'm getting through to him. All my texts aren't just going into a bit bucket. He's reading them. It's all just going over his tiny little brain. As evidenced by another try with DateYou that evening. He did take it up a notch though, using "46g77146," a password DateYou was kind enough to email me, saving me the trouble of resetting the password before going in to delete the account. Again.

Even though he had filled in next to nothing on his profile, there were soon 40 messages waiting for him from various girls supposedly intrigued by it and wondering why he hadn't gotten back to them. Just like all the other dating sites, these girls, or more appropriately, customer service agents, as there's no guarantee they're even female, are probably paid on commission to get the Colemans of the world to pony up what little cash they have for an upgraded (i.e., paid) membership. With a free membership, they give you just enough to whet your appetite, but in order to "date" any of these agents, you have to dig out your credit card.

Now, of course, no one is forcing anyone to give out their credit card information. It's all completely voluntary. No crime is being committed. Still, it's sad on all counts that this "industry" is obviously thriving by preying on the likes of David Coleman.

Friday, January 31

David Coleman is slowing down.

But he's not done. Not by a long shot.

Each of the last two days has seen Coleman sign up for a new dating site. Today's was Chubby Soulmate, as he returns to the BBW theme, which seems to be his favorite.

Sunday, February 2

Overnight, David Coleman tried to sign up at WellHello again.

That marks his 26th such attempt.

But at least it was just the one today. He seems to be limiting himself to one or two sites per day. As if he were on a diet or a recovering smoker.

Monday, February 3

David Coleman tried two old sites today.

Early in the morning, he went back to DateYou for the sixth time and 12 minutes later, he tried to reset the password to get into the Chubby Soulmate account he created that I locked him out of. Too bad for him the link came to me and not to him.

Wednesday, February 5

David Coleman took a break from the dating sites to tend to his ailing finances.

Overnight, he tried again with a bill-payment service that he first signed me up for in early October that I had to extricate myself from. No doubt he still had the app on his phone and was determined to get in. So this time, I logged in and rerouted the account to Isabella, the "woman" I had Coleman pining for, and unlinked it from my email address.

Thursday, February 6

David Coleman is still around.

Around the noon hour, he tried DateYou for the seventh time. He also used a unique password, "2e0zc6w8."

He knows something's wrong. He just can't figure out what it is.

I know what the problem is.

It's what's between his ears.

Tuesday, February 11

David Coleman had been quiet for five days.

I was beginning to wonder what happened to him.

I had even searched through the obituaries in his area to see if he had passed away.

But I wondered no longer when I got the notification that he signed up with DateYou for the eighth time. This time, he didn't bother coming up with anything unique and just went back to his usual password. He did, however, enter a different birth date. Maybe that will be the difference. Or not.

Less than a half hour later, he signed me up at a new site, OurSecretFlirts. Those "secret flirts" obviously aren't too secret since he's quite willing to share them with a perfect stranger.

Wednesday, February 12

David Coleman is obsessed with WellHello.

In the afternoon, he tried for the 27th time, only to be foiled yet again by that pesky email verification scheme they have. For all I know, he might even have emailed their support desk to complain about it.

I keep wondering how he has enough brain power to sign up to these sites. He reminds me of an Alzheimer's or a dementia patient sitting in a nursing home who keeps forgetting that his wife died and is unable to recognize other family members. Except that he's only in his 30s. Maybe it's a case of drugs or drinking binges.

Saturday, February 15

Overnight, David Coleman tried something different.

He attempted to create a membership with a place called the Honor Society. Except that he can only activate it with the email they sent me.

Dear David,

Congratulations! You are invited to join the Honor Society professional network. Accepting this distinction connects you with like-minded high achievers from your region and across the nation, both in person and through our society's web portal. Our network helps connect you with leaders from high profile universities and employers across the nation.

Honor Society is the preeminent organization dedicated to recognition of academic and professional success. Our society empowers members to achieve through scholarship, recognition, exclusive privileges, job opportunities and much more. Honor Society recognizes your achievements to date, and builds a framework for future success.

Featured Privileges

Exclusive Scholarship Listings
Full Access to Career Insider Guide books and tools by Vault.com (up to $1,000 value)
Dental, Vision and Hearing Health Discount Plans valid at 200,000 access points nationwide
Honor Society regalia - honor cords & tassels
Dining discounts at 18,000 restaurant nationwide

Graduation Regalia & Honor Cords
Honor Society regalia is available exclusively for Honor Society members. Display your recognition and member standing with the double stranded royal blue and gold themed honor cords, stoles and medallions of Honor Society on your graduation day, or for a keepsake.

David Coleman a high achiever? I don't think so.

Monday, February 17

Increasingly desperate, David Coleman continues to sift through the archives.

This morning, he tried again at ComeWithYou, a place he hadn't tried since late October.

Checking the site as I went in to delete the account, I noticed that they even accept couples. Two credit cards are better than one, I suppose.

Tuesday, February 18

David Coleman tried another old site today.

This time, he signed me up at Meetmilfy for the second time following his first attempt with them in early January. He did upload a new selfie. He's capable of that much. But he still can't figure out that the email address he's been hammering away on for the past six months isn't his.

In the evening, I got this from Larters Bank:

From: Larters Bank
Subject: Start growing your savings even faster
To: David Coleman

Make your money grow faster

Hi David,

You work hard for your money. Now, we're making it work harder for you.

*Your Larters Savings Account now earns 1.60% Annual Percentage Yield (APY) —
that's more than 17x the national average!*

*This is a variable rate and may change. We always try to give you the highest rate
possible.*

*On top of a great interest rate, you still enjoy these great Larters Savings Account
features:*

Grow your savings automatically

*Set money aside with Automatic Savings features like Round Ups and Save When I
Get Paid.*

No fees. No catch. No worries.

*One simple rate. No minimum balance requirement, no maximums on interest earned.
And no fees.*

Secure and FDIC insured

*We use encryption and secure processes to help ensure your money is safe. Deposits are
insured through our partners, The Bancorp Bank or Stride Bank, Members FDIC.*

Ready to start earning more with your money? Move money into Savings!

So I sent this off in response, not just to try to stop these emails, but in the hopes that they'll contact Coleman and buy me a few days of freedom.

I am the legitimate owner of the email address david82@FreeAMail.net, the one a David Coleman of Deland, FL has used to open an account. As this address belongs to me and not Mr. Coleman, please remove this UNVERIFIED address from his records and STOP sending any further communication to that address.

Your emails always state that "you're receiving this email because you are a Larters Bank customer" yet I have never done business with Larters and have not verified the email address Mr. Coleman gave you.

I further urge Larters to modify its security procedures and not send personal information (address and phone number) to unverified email addresses, as you have done with Mr. Coleman.

Wednesday, February 19

If Larters Bank indeed contacted David Coleman, their words went in one ear and out the other.

Because later in the afternoon, he found another dating site to sign me up for. Join us and find your couple, they say.

In his profile, he stated that he's interested in communication with people who have strong family values, who have kids, who are looking for a penfriend, who want to have fun, who are looking for a friend and who want to flirt. His ideal body type for women is "a few extra pounds, Big & beautiful."

And stupid. Just like him.

Sunday, February 23

David Coleman was again kind enough to give me a few days off.

But he was back at it early this morning, trying again with old sites he had first tried in late November.

He's desperate, all right.

But not desperate enough to use his own email address instead of mine.

Wednesday, February 26

David Coleman seems to be giving up the battle.

But there's still a lot of fight left in the guy.

This evening, after another lull, he tried again at DateYou, marking his ninth such attempt.

While online disposing of the account, I got a message from one of their agents, who encouraged me to come out and see who's behind that profile. Needless to say, I didn't bite, though it would have been tempting to humor him or her. The agent doesn't know how lucky he or she was, because if it had been Coleman, all he would have done is waste their time. After all, they're only after his money, of which he has very little.

And even less brains.

Tuesday, March 3

It had been almost a full week since David Coleman signed me up for anything.

I thought it might have slowly started sinking in that he had been using someone else's email address.

That is, until he tried DateYou for the 10th time.

He's not ready to give up yet.

Wednesday, March 4

David Coleman is back on the prowl.

This evening, he tried again at ezhookups. Interested in casual dating for sex, but don't know where to start, they ask? We guarantee that you will meet lonely cheating wives and possibly get laid as early as TONIGHT! Find the best sex hookups in your city. Discover the top sex hookups for you.

Yeah, whatever.

Only someone as dumb as Coleman could fall for that shit.

For good measure, I heard again from Kilton University, kindly informing me of their upcoming open house, even though I had unsubscribed from their general mailings and contacted two of their admissions reps to ask them to stop spamming me.

So I tried again.

Hello. I am the legitimate owner of david82@FreeAMail.net, the email address David Coleman of Deland mistakenly gave you.

I have previously emailed two different admissions reps at Kilton informing them that address doesn't belong to Mr. Coleman and asking them to remove that address from his file and stop all further communication to that address.

Once again, I insist you remove the email address david82@FreeAMail.net from Mr. Coleman's file and STOP ALL FURTHER COMMUNICATION to that address.

Perhaps the third time will be a charm.

Thursday, March 5

David Coleman is getting back in the swing of things.

Overnight, he found a new dating site to sign me up for, and early in the morning, he tried another one that he first tried in late November.

Then I got another email from Kilton University. Those people are proving to be just as persistent as Coleman himself.

From: Angela Bishop
Subject: An Important Message from KILTON UNIVERSITY
To: David Coleman

Dear David,

We have attempted to reach you several times via phone regarding your interest in Kilton University's career opportunities.

It's not too late! We are actively enrolling for our upcoming start!

Please contact me so that I may assist you.

Thank you for your interest!

Sincerely,

Angela Bishop
Admissions Counselor
Kilton University

So I responded to Angela. This time, I wasn't nearly as polite as I was the first time.

Angela, enough is enough. As I have previously indicated to you and others at Kilton University, this is not the address for David Coleman, who mistakenly gave you my email address of david82@FreeAMail.net.

Let me spell it out more clearly for you.

REMOVE   DAVID82@FREEAMAIL.NET   FROM   DAVID COLEMAN'S FILE.

STOP SENDING EMAILS TO DAVID82@FREEAMAIL.NET.

Maybe now you'll listen.

I only regret not using stronger wording.

Friday, March 6

No rest for the wicked.

Overnight, David Coleman signed up at DateYou for the 11th time and once again at NaughtyDate. It's such a shame that he's missed out on the six yummy girls who liked his profile and the private message from Deonna.

So much for the "he's slowly starting to figure it out" theory.

Sadly, Larters Bank is also going on a rampage as they sent me another email, this time telling me that the interest rate on Coleman's savings account is going down.

Obviously they didn't get the message the first time. So I fired back with another message of my own. Actually, nine of them. If they're going to recklessly spam me, I'm going to return the favor. Maybe that will get their attention.

I am the legitimate owner of the email address david82@FreeAMail.net. As I previously explained, this unverified address was given to you mistakenly by David Coleman of Deland, FL. Yet even though I am not a Larters customer nor do I have a Larters account as you claim, you continue to spam an UNVERIFIED EMAIL ADDRESS with messages like these.

Therefore, until you stop spamming me, I will continue to spam you.

One thing I'm discovering through all of this is that it's not just Coleman or the sleazy dating sites that are the problem. So many legitimate companies who get a hold of your email address just won't let it go.

Saturday, March 7

David Coleman is back, and with a vengeance.

In the morning, he signed me up for HotTalks, a site that provides daily update emails for information on meeting others. Emails like this:

Hey again,

Here's a fun little quiz:

If girls were donuts, what kind of donut would you want?

Glazed donuts represent girls who are sweet and simple.

They're loyal to a fault, and you can count on them, too -- just like you know that no matter what, your favorite donut shop will always be stocked with glazed donuts.

What about the other types of "donuts?"

Here, have a look:

Coconut - a summer fling sort of girl who's adventurous, different, and exciting. She loves having fun and lives in the moment.

Munchkin - pretty traditional woman when it comes to dating. She appreciates it when you pay for the date, open the door for her, and so on

Sprinkle - she's sweet, fun, a littl quirky, and makes you feel young-at-heart

Chocolate cake - some people love chocolate with a passion, and others dislike it. Similarly, this donut represents a girl who is fiercely passionate, and if you like her, you'll REALLY like her. Other guys are attracted to her, too

Thought I'd share this exercise with you to get you thinking about what kind of girl you want to end up with -- or sleep with.

And if you don't know what you're looking for?

No worries, man.

The world is yours to explore, and that includes women, too.

Start that exploration of yours by going to this site.

Taylor S

Soon after, an agent replied to a message he sent.

Lucky You! Alexis1992bx Replied to Your Message...

Hi there - You guessed that I am secretly naughty. Very shy out in public but discreet and thrilling when it's just us! If you know the way to have fun with a girl like me, please respond quickly as I am in need to release myself!

Do people really fall for this shit?

Moving on, around the noon hour, he got hungry. So he signed me up for Pizza Hut Rewards and ordered a pizza shortly thereafter. One large original pan pizza, classic marinara sauce, pepperoni and Italian sausage, which set him back $19.36. He gave his usual mobile number, but had it delivered to a different address. Perhaps he was visiting a friend. Or maybe he moved. I logged in to see if I could change the order, just to screw with him, but all I could do without calling them was change the password to lock him out of the rewards program.

I also made sure to tell him.

Hey Coleman, try logging into your/my Pizza Hut Rewards account now. Go ahead. I double-dog dare ya!

Hey Coleman, you know there's really something wrong with you. Seek professional help. Now.

Sunday, March 8

David Coleman is the gift that keeps on giving.

He tried twice more with DateYou, and in between his 12th and 13th attempts, he tried seekmeetdate again, prompting a couple of more texts from me.

Hey Coleman, here's a tip. You want to get on dateyou so bad? USE YOUR OWN EMAIL ADDRESS!!!

Tell me Coleman, are you on drugs? Or maybe you're a dementia patient?

He's just flailing away.

He doesn't know what to do.

But the only thing he hasn't done differently is exactly what his and my problem is.

He's still using my email address instead of his own.

Monday, March 9

David Coleman remains as thick-headed as ever.

Early in the morning, he signed up for another new dating site before trying DateYou again in the afternoon, bringing the tally to 14. Another Nintendo.

In between, Kilton University sent me another promotional email. Obviously I'm still on file with them. I think they're just as thick-headed as Coleman is.

Thursday, March 12

David Coleman took a little time off.

But he's back in business once again.

Continuing to defy all rational logic, he made his 28th attempt to get on WellHello. Prompting more texts from me.

Every account you create under my credentials (david82-at-freeamail.net) is mine, not yours
I will delete every such account you create, do you understand?
I will continue to defend your aggressive assault on my inbox

Tuesday, March 17

My last communication seemed to have an effect on David Coleman.

But it didn't last.

Going back to chapter 1, he tried again at Snapchat, this time using the user ID of sidneyyy120v8w8 and a different password.

Once again, I unlinked the account from my email address.

If only I could unlink Coleman from my life.

Wednesday, March 18

It's back to the dating sites for David Coleman.

In the afternoon, he tried InstantHookups again, a site he first tried in late December. Forcing me once again to go in, using the user ID and password they were nice enough to send along, and log in so I could delete the account.

Thursday, March 19

Nothing more from David Coleman today.

But sadly, Larters Bank is proving to be just as obnoxious as Coleman.

During the day, they sent me a notification stating that the interest rate on his zero-balance savings account is changing again. So I sent them 21 copies of this:

I am the legitimate owner of david82@FreeAMail.net, the email address David Coleman of Deland, Florida gave you.

As I have previously and repeatedly explained to Larters, this address does not belong to Mr. Coleman and as this address has not been verified, you have no business spamming me.

I demand that you remove my email address from your files and stop this spam at once.

For good measure, I added a few more copies of this later in the day:

I am the legitimate owner of david82@FreeAMail.net.

This address that's on your files is UNVERIFIED.

I am not a Larters Bank customer.
Thus, I demand to be removed from your spam list.

STOP SPAMMING ME.

P.S.: You folks don't like getting spammed? Guess what, neither do I.

Friday, March 20

David Coleman likes pizza.

And he's determined to get it.

So, after having struck out at Domino's and Pizza Hut, he tried to create an account with Little Caesars. Too bad for him that, unlike those other two, Little Caesars requires email verification.

So I sent this off to him:

Hey Coleman, got your verification email for Little Caesars.
You want pizza from them? USE YOUR OWN EMAIL ADDRESS!!!!

Sunday, March 22

Unable to create an account with them, David Coleman pursued another angle with Little Caesars.

He signed up for the "Little Caesars Nation" email list, forcing me to unsubscribe. If only they were as nice about insisting on email verification with that as they were about creating an account.

Monday, March 23

This just in. David Coleman doesn't give up easily.

Overnight, he tried again at DateYou.

That made 15 such attempts.

So I sent the following off to him. Maybe it will spook him and buy me a few days of peace. It's worth a try.

Hey Coleman, just got rid of your latest DateYou account.
I repeat – I will delete every account you create under my credentials (david82-at-freeamail.net).

Tuesday, March 24

Today brought something completely new from David Coleman.

This time, he signed up for emails at the U.S. Concealed Carry Association, promoting membership in the best association for those looking to keep themselves and the people they love safe.

The thought of Coleman with a gun is scary. I support gun rights and all, but he's living proof that there ought to be an IQ test before you can get one. It could be as simple as one question.

What's your email address?

Wednesday, March 25

David Coleman still wants to quit smoking.

So he again signed up for a quit smoking group through Tobacco Free Florida.

But what he really needs is a support group for people hopelessly addicted to using someone else's email address.

Which is exactly what I told him in a text.

If only it would sink in.

Friday, March 27

After a day off, David Coleman went back to an old favorite.

Early in the morning, he made his 29th attempt at WellHello.

Equally troubling as Coleman is Kilton University, who sent me another invitation to an open house. Time and again, I've emailed them, clicked every unsubscribe link and they *still* haven't taken me off their files.

At least Coleman has an excuse. He's just stupid.

Kilton University is supposed to be a place of higher education.

Presumably, you have to be a little brighter than a sheet of drywall to work there.

No End in Sight

Thursday, April 2

David Coleman gave me almost a week off.

But every so often, he has to let me know he's around.

Like this morning, when he signed me up at MomsGetNaughty.

This time, he even took the time to upload a new selfie. From the background, the shot matches up exactly with the images on Google Earth from the address where he had the pizza delivered. Perhaps he's moved there.

I should send him a housewarming gift.

Friday, April 3

No activity from David Coleman today.

But I did hear from Larters Bank, an outfit nearly as obnoxious as Coleman.

Once again, they were nice enough to tell me that the interest rate on his zero-balance savings account was changing.

So I sent another missive off to them, 17 of them to be exact.

I am the legitimate owner of david82@FreeAMail.net, the UNVERIFIED email address David Coleman of Deland gave you.

For the umpteenth time, I am not a Larters customer.

Mr. Coleman has a Larters savings account. I do not.

Thus, I demand to have my email address removed from your files.

Sunday, April 5

David Coleman keeps digging up old dating sites from the archives.

This time, he tried OneNightFriend again.

He's sure not my friend.

And this has been going on for a lot longer than one night.

Saturday, April 11

David Coleman nearly made it a full week without any activity.

But then he fell off the wagon.

He tried one more time with WellHello. The 30th attempt is second only to Nintendo in his hall of shame.

Monday, April 13

Two more dating sites for David Coleman today, just over an hour apart.

Checking online, the first of the two got a particularly scathing review. They ask for credit card information right away, ostensibly as an age verification measure to protect and prevent minors from joining, then they promptly begin dinging your card at three different sites to the tune of $120 per month. Not surprisingly, the reviewer also found that the profile pictures of their "girls" had been taken from porno sites. Pictures that most often show the girls naked or in bikinis. As the reviewer stated, this is done to lure men into upgrading to paid memberships because they start thinking with their little head and not their big head.

Coleman doesn't know how lucky he is that he used someone else's email address. And that he doesn't have a credit card to give them.

Wednesday, April 15

Another pair of old dating sites for David Coleman today.

Overnight, he tried again at Flirt.com and in the afternoon, he tried DateYou for the 16th time.

Someone recently suggested to me that I pick up the phone and call him. Sure, I know his number, along with just about every other detail of his personal life. But if all those texts, emails from me and calls from people he's talked to can't get through to him, my words aren't going to mean a whole lot either.

Saturday, April 18

Striking out so often with WellHello, David Coleman is now fixated on DateYou.

Overnight, he tried them for the 17th time, forcing me into an all-too-familiar routine of logging in and deleting the account.

Too bad there isn't some automated way of doing this. Being exposed to all this filth is sickening.

Sunday, April 19

Still more activity in the wee hours of the morning for David Coleman.

Maybe he's been spending a lot of time partying with drugs and/or alcohol.

First was SensualMeets, then he made another attempt at InstantHookups. Later in the day, he found another new site, MeetMe. Chat and meet new people, they say. Which is pretty tough when you don't give them your own email address.

Perhaps the only reason for that lull a while ago was that he was busy moving. And now that he's settled at his new place, he's again got time on his hands to try to find a dating site that will accept him at "his" email address.

Wednesday, April 22

David Coleman went on another rampage today.

He signed up with four dating sites within the span of two hours. TrueBootyCall was the first. Hook up with hot girls and get off online, they say. Then it was CheatingDates. They offer 30 free flirts to get suckers like Coleman going with one of their agents before you have to give them your credit card. After that was FreeLocalDates. "Like sex all day long and fun" was what he had to say in his profile. While navigating through the site to find the option to delete the account, agents kept popping up trying to initiate conversation. So often I was tempted to answer, "Get lost, bitch!" One featured a .gif showing a scantily clad girl flashing a credit card and entering the number on her keyboard. That's what this shit is really all about for them. Finally, he tried Flirt.com again.

After cleaning up the mess, I sent Coleman a couple of more memes featuring his most recent selfie. One had the caption "I keep signing up to websites using someone else's email address and I can't figure out why I never get any responses." On the next one, I used "Dumbest. Human. Ever."

One of these days, something's bound to click.

Thursday, April 23

I get the feeling David Coleman spends all his waking hours these days searching for dating sites.

Because today, he found two more new ones to sign up for.

Early in the morning, he signed up at LustSeek, a site that offers paid members the opportunity to "find local cheaters." While online trying to dispose of the account, I got hammered by agents looking for action. Late in the day, he signed me up at WantMatures. Coleman might want someone mature, but no mature adult would want him.

Mixed in there was a game he signed me up for. As they didn't allow me to log in via the website, I had to download the app on my tablet so I could go in and reset the password to lock him out and stop the email alerts.

Friday, April 24

An action-packed day began with an invitation to an online meeting from Francisco Barrios of Tobacco Free Florida.

Then when I didn't respond, he fired off another reminder email.

In both cases, he also listed all nine recipients in the "To" field. How courteous of him.

So I sent this in reply:

Francisco, I am the legitimate owner of david82@FreeAMail.net, the address David Coleman of Deland mistakenly provided to Tobacco Free Florida as his own. Please remove my address from your files and send me no more communication.

Furthermore, I strongly urge you to be more discreet when sending out mass emails and use the "Bcc" feature.

Thank you.

Following this, Coleman sprang into action, trying again at WellHello and DateYou a half hour apart. It marked his 31st attempt with the former and the 18th with the latter.

So I sent him the following:

Hey Coleman, got rid of the latest account you created for me at DateYou.
I also locked you out of that game last night.
You're a pretty slow learner aren't you?

Unfazed, within a two-hour interval, he signed up at PickYourFling and tried again with QuickFlirt. Before the day was out, he signed up at a cross-dressing site. Welcome to America's local cross-dresser dating site, they say. Everyone is welcome here, whether you are a cross-dresser or an admirer, we have members that are ready to explore. Arrange cross-dresser meets in your zip code and in different states across the country. If you have a desire to date transsexuals, find friendships or have naughty hookups, you will find someone to have fun with here.

He also took the time to answer their questionnaire.

The first question was "What erotic fun do you want to have here?" Of the available options, he chose group sex, long-term regular meets, adult chat and anal sex, while saying no to sexual roleplay, threesomes and BDSM.

For "What will our members do to get you horny," he chose undress me, take pictures of me, give a catwalk, admire me and strip on webcam. He didn't care for the dress me or share clothes options.

When it came time to select his turn-ons, he chose pantyhose and showing off. Latex, suspenders, lace, men dressing as women, women dressing as men and public dress-up apparently did nothing for him.

Finally, he didn't care much about the age group. Basically, anyone 60 and under would do.

He was so desperate to get on that site that he asked for a second verification email five minutes after first signing up.

To say the least, Coleman really scraped the bottom of the barrel with this one. But even a site like this will remain beyond his grasp until he provides his own email address. Something he appears to be utterly incapable of figuring out.

Saturday, April 25

It was a relatively quiet day on the David Coleman front.

All that came through my inbox was a pair of verification requests for

BetterHelp, a site that offers professional counseling with licensed therapists. You deserve to be happy, they say. I certainly can't blame Coleman for being down in the dumps after striking out so often with all the websites he's been signing me up to. Too bad he repeated his mistake by signing up using my email address once again, because they actually insisted on entering a verification code before continuing. So, in other words, he can't get the counseling he needs because of the same problem that's causing his depression.

Soon after, I sent this off to him:

Hey Coleman, looking for counseling? Must be getting depressing striking out so often. Here's a tip: Use your own email address.

Sunday, April 26

David Coleman may still be depressed.

But he's not depressed enough to stop signing up with dating sites using my email address.

Late in the day, he tried DateYou again before signing up at a couple of new sites. Just finding new ones must be a hell of a challenge these days.

So I sent him another meme, this one featuring Batman slapping Robin. After Robin said, "I signed up using david82@FreeAMail.net . . .," Batman slaps him across the face and says, "You idiot! Stop using someone else's email address!"

Unfortunately, I doubt that Coleman will find it funny.

Monday, April 27

David Coleman continues to keep me busy.

Overnight, he made another attempt at MaturesForFuck.

Later in the morning, I got another email from Francisco Barrios of Tobacco Free Florida, where he again revealed all the email addresses of the recipients of his mass email, prompting this reply:

Francisco, I am the legitimate owner of david82@FreeAMail.net. As I previously explained to you, I did not sign up with Tobacco Free Florida. As such, I demand you stop sending me these emails.

I am also outraged at your continued indiscretion at not using the "bcc" feature for these mass emails which I am involuntarily part of.

Hold yourself to a higher standard, sir.

A couple of hours later, I got a pair of emails from him, just to me, with no content, but with the subject stating that the online session had been canceled. Hopefully that means I'm off the list.

Shortly thereafter, Coleman tried again at WellHello for the 32nd time.

That evening, Coleman turned his attention back to money matters. Seven minutes apart, he signed up for newsletters at Eligibility Assistance and at Online Financial Assistance, both nongovernmental entities. After all, a sporadically employed moron does need to think about these things in order to fund his smoking, drinking and drug habits and for online dating. That is, assuming he can ever get past that nagging stickler of a question.

What's your email address?

Tuesday, April 28

David Coleman was back in action bright and early this morning.

An hour and a half apart, he tried two recent dating sites I had previously extricated myself from. And had to do so once again. Two hours later, he switched gears and signed up for a newsletter at Section 8 Assistance, then it was back to the dating sites, signing up for SteamyDates and SimpleFlirts 17 minutes apart.

Minutes later, Francisco Barrios at Tobacco Free Florida sent me another online meeting invitation. So I sent this in reply:

For the third time, I didn't sign up for this. STOP SENDING ME THIS SHIT!

This is how he responded:

I received your email from, and I just spoke to the person that did registered for the program and verified his email. I don't know what is going on and why your response comes from and unverified email.

Um, whatever.

Moving on, rather than continue with the anonymous email service with disposable addresses I had been using to communicate with Coleman, I decided to create an actual account with a free service and use it instead. Just to be able to see if he replies.

And I began by sending the following:

Hey Coleman, sorry to hear that your finances are in the crapper.
But if you really want assistance, maybe you should consider USING YOUR OWN EMAIL ADDRESS, ASSHOLE!
Come to think of it, maybe you might get more success in your love life too if you used your own email address instead of mine.
Guess you don't have anything better to do than to sign me up at dating sites and benefit mailing lists.
Tell me Coleman, hasn't it dawned on you that you're using the wrong email address?
Even someone as dumb as you ought to be able to figure it out.
You've tried, what, 32 times at WellHello now?

Then I added this:

Hey Coleman, congratulations on your move.
Thanks for sending me the address when you ordered at Pizza Hut.
Something to consider: Don't like getting all these texts? Guess what, I don't like getting all your shit either.

And sure enough, he did respond.

Sorry what's up
I just woke up

So, now with a two-way line of communication established, I sent this:

You asshole! Just got rid of the SteamyDates and SimpleFlirts accounts.
Pretty slow learner, aren't you?
Tell me, Coleman, are you on drugs?

He responded as follows:

No I don't use any drugs
What are you doing now
If I can ask

No, I don't use any drugs. Yeah, right.
I then sent this off:

Hey asshole! What part of "david82-at-freeamail.net doesn't belong to you" do you not
understand?
I repeat. I will delete each and every account you create under my credentials (david82-
at-freeamail.net).
I will defend myself against your relentless assault on my inbox.

Coleman took about an hour to process all this before signing me up at a pair of transsexual dating sites two minutes apart. He's really getting hard up. But not hard up enough to start using his own email address.

So I sent more off to him:

Hey Coleman, you jackass. Didn't know you were into transsexuals.
I just deleted the Local Trans Dating and TSDates accounts you signed me up for.
You want online dating? USE YOUR OWN EMAIL ADDRESS!!!

Thursday, April 30

Tuesday's exchange bought me a day off from David Coleman.

But early in the morning, he got right back in the saddle, trying DateYou for the 20th time. This time, he uploaded a new selfie he took in a dark, narrow hallway with some food stuck on the side of his mouth. Yuck.

So I sent off the following:

Hey Coleman, just got rid of the latest DateYou account you created for me.
Put down the drugs, Coleman. No one could be this stupid otherwise.

And a couple of hours later, he responded.

Ok
What's up
I'm still up

This guy really is a moron.

Friday, May 1

Perhaps spooked, David Coleman gave me a 24-hour break.

Then he signed up with Lyft. I guess he needs a ride to go somewhere. At least they gave me the option to remove my email address from the account.

Later in the afternoon, I got an email from American Student Assistance. Coleman had apparently called them asking for information on how to apply for federal student aid, something he had previously applied for. I was shocked that I didn't know that because surely he would have given my email address.

Whatever the case, I was at least relieved he had signed up for something that wasn't a dating site.

These days, that constitutes a victory where Coleman is concerned.

Nonetheless, I sent him the following soon after:

Hey Coleman, if you want student assistance, try giving them your email address instead of mine.

This is how he responded:

Ok
What's up

Stupid is as stupid does.

Saturday, May 2

David Coleman's wallet must be getting a little light.

Because for the first time in a while, he seems to be more worried about jobs and money than finding someone to talk dirty to online.

Early in the morning, he asked for information from Unemployment Information Center and from Skills and Careers. Then in the afternoon, I heard from a law office that Coleman had apparently been speaking with specializing in repairing credit. Minutes later, he created an account with them using my email address. Naturally, like so many others, they didn't ask for verification, nor did they allow me to reset the password. Bastards.

But despite all his financial worries, the man still needs to eat. So late in the day, he signed me up at McDonald's through their app. Or at least he tried to, since the verification email, as always, came to me and not to him.

Breakthrough

Sunday, May 3

David Coleman never ceases to amaze me.

Because he found yet another new dating site to sign me up for.

Bright and early, he created an account at PassionMature and even took the time to upload a recent selfie, something I discovered while deleting the account.

This prompted the following exchange:

Coleman, you asshole!
Just got rid of the latest account you created for me.
Use your own email address, you retard!

What's up

You retard! You shouldn't be allowed anywhere near a computer!

Morning beautiful

Screw you Coleman!
Tell me Coleman, do you ever wonder why you always run into problems when you use my email address?
Is there that little between your ears?
Understand this, Coleman — you keep filling my inbox with your shit, I'll keep filling yours.

Switching back to money matters, just after noon, Coleman applied for a checking account with Stage One Bank. And, of course, they sent me the code to view the status of his application. Something I made sure to tell him.

Hey Coleman, just got your Stage One application code.
Guess you didn't think to send it your email address instead of mine.
God, you're a moron!

This seemed to grab his attention as he responded right away. Normally, there had been significant lag times between his replies.

Lol
Call me
7865557546

Maybe it's just me, but I wouldn't find it funny that a perfect stranger has access to my checking account application code.

But then again, I'm not David Coleman.

And aren't I lucky.

Later in the afternoon, I got an email from an online streaming service giving a privacy policy update. We make it easy and affordable to watch your favorite TV shows, they say. Watch what you love for less. Nothing from them had crossed my inbox before, but when I went to their site and tried to log in using my email address and Coleman's favorite password, sure enough, I got in. So now these places aren't even bothering to send a notification when someone creates an account using your email address. But I did get a notification when I changed the password and chose the "log out of all devices" option before deleting the account entirely.

As I've long since discovered, corporate America has a long way to go with respect to email etiquette.

Monday, May 4

History was made today.

This afternoon, David Coleman's checking account application was approved.

That's right, Coleman is the proud owner of a Stage One Bank checking account.

No doubt, it had to have been the lawyer's intervention. And he must have been awfully persuasive. I'll be sure to keep him in mind if I run into financial difficulties.

Stage One then wanted him to confirm his (my) email address. Not that the lack of verification stopped them from firing off an avalanche of emails telling me that his account has a $10.00 monthly service fee, waived if he maintains a $1,500 balance, and that he ordered a Consumer Platinum Debit Card, which should be arriving in the mail within five to seven days.

So I gave Coleman the Cliff's Notes version. I'm sure he'd want to know.

Hey Coleman, heard more from Stage One.
They want me to confirm my email address.
I won't.
You need to give them YOUR email address, not mine, you retard.

He didn't respond. But 11 minutes later, he did add a new email address to his file. He didn't remove mine, of course, but this was the first real sign that he might be starting to get the hint. Maybe, just maybe, he might even start connecting the dots a little more when he starts getting emails at the other account and not at mine.

But alas, less than an hour later, I got an email from TD Bank saying that Coleman didn't complete his checking account application. He had tried with them back in September, but perhaps, thinking he was on a roll, he tried to make it two for two. But again, as always, he failed the all-important first question. What's your email address? Something I made sure to tell him.

Hey Coleman, heard from TD Bank. They say you didn't complete your checking acct application.
You also gave them my email address instead of yours, you retard!

Tuesday, May 5

Today, I got a weekly mailing from a motorcycle shop.

Not surprisingly, the shop is located near David Coleman's home.

I took the liberty of assuming he was behind it, though I have no idea when he actually signed me up for the list. Fortunately, they allowed me to easily unsubscribe.

I found it interesting that he used the address david.82@FreeAMail.net instead of david82@FreeAMail.net.

Like that's going to make all the difference.

Wednesday, May 6

Early this morning, Stage One Bank was kind enough to tell me that David

Coleman's debit card has been shipped.

I had hoped he might have taken it a step further and removed my email address from his file. But obviously, he hadn't.

So I sent this off to him:

Hey Coleman, heard about your Stage One debit card.

Also got the email from your motorcycle shop. Looks like you signed me up for another list.

Pretty slow learner, aren't you Coleman?

Monday, May 11

Nothing new on the David Coleman front.

Except that I'm still on file with Stage One.

This evening, I got a promotional email from them and promptly unsubscribed.

Too bad they won't let me unsubscribe from Coleman's account. An account I should never have been part of in the first place.

Tuesday, May 19

Just when I began to get optimistic that David Coleman might be in my past, he reared his ugly head once again.

This time, he gave my email address when placing an order at Chili's. He ordered a Chicky Chicky Bleu Sandwich with mayonnaise, one order of Crispy Chicken Crispers with ranch dressing and two side orders of fries, one order of Original Chicken Crispers with two side orders of fries and one order of Pepper Pals Crispy Crispers with mandarin oranges. And he'll try to wash that all down with a Coke. Not Pepsi. Because Coke is the real thing apparently. The big shocker of the $48.98 order, however, was the payment method. Visa. Surely Coleman couldn't have gotten a credit card, even a prepaid one. And even if he did, how did I not know about it? But then again, thinking about it a little more, one person, even chubby Coleman, couldn't possibly eat all that. He's probably planning a party, and the Visa card probably belongs to one of the guests. Makes perfect sense. Invite people to a party at your house and have the guests pay for the food.

Sadly, there was no option to change or cancel the order without calling the restaurant directly. I thought about doing just that, but I couldn't be bothered. It was awfully tempting though.

Wednesday, May 27

Fortunately, David Coleman keeps getting farther and farther off my radar.

But he still can't help himself from using my email address. I'm hoping it's just a case of muscle memory.

Overnight, he signed me up at EliteSingles again, a place he first signed up with in early November. As before, I had to go through this 99-page "scientific personality test" before I could get into the settings. Except that this time, unlike before, there was no option there to delete the account, forcing me to contact their support desk to dispose of it.

If only they made it just as difficult to sign up as they do to rid yourself of these accounts.

Slowly Letting Go

Tuesday, June 9

Old habits are hard to break for David Coleman.

This morning, a notification popped up in my inbox to reset my password at Kinkoo App. The most innovative kinky dating app for open-minded people who are into fetish and BDSM lifestyle, they say. More and more people are getting into kinky life because of the popularity of some BDSM movies. However, it's not easy for kinksters to find like-minded partners. Few people would like to tell others that they are looking for kinky partners on their dating profiles because of the social stigma towards people who are into kinks.

This is another place that didn't even bother to tell me that Coleman had used my email address to sign up for an account. But nonetheless, I took advantage of the opportunity to reset the password to lock him out. I'd have happily taken it a step further and deleted the account entirely if only I could have done so via the website. In order to get in, you've got to download their app. And damned if I'm going to soil my tablet with their app.

Monday, June 15

Even though he seems to be slowly coming to the realization that my email address isn't his, David Coleman just can't help himself.

Overnight, he signed me up at an especially sleazy dating site, one that he first tried back in September. From the IP address they provided, I knew it was definitely him. Too bad for him they emailed me the system-generated user ID and password, but when I logged in to try to delete the account, they wouldn't let me get anywhere without upgrading to a "free lifetime membership." All I had to do was provide them with my credit card information to verify that I was over 18. Coleman might be that stupid, but I'm not.

Wednesday, June 17

Repeat after me. It's just muscle memory. It's just muscle memory.

David Coleman signed me up at QuickFlirt overnight.

That's the fourth time he's tried there.

To borrow a line from one of the *Rambo* movies, the boy is resilient.

When I logged in to delete the account, I saw that 44 agents liked his profile. Agents such as LittleDynamitexx and Libby1. There were also 18 messages from agents like Lanessa, Jenn and Chrissie7567. But even if he had used his own email address, he would have needed to have upgraded his membership (i.e., pay) to read them. And if he didn't do it in two hours' time, the messages would have been deleted. My heart bleeds.

He even took the time to upload a new selfie. He took the shot from behind his block in the setting sun while wearing a Superman cap. Super stupid is more like it. He also trimmed up his beard a little and cleaned the snot out of his nose. Improved personal grooming habits can't hurt when trying to curry favor with agents of the opposite sex.

Thursday, June 18

Early this morning, Stage One Bank offered me the opportunity to take part in a survey.

Stage One is always striving to improve their customers' experience, they say. So I took the bait.

When it came time to give the reasons why David Coleman's new Stage One checking account is not my primary checking account, I told them. Same thing when they asked about the confirmation email regarding the status of his application.

That's because I'm not a Stage One customer. Someone else opened an account with them and gave my email address, which Stage One did not verify before spamming the living daylights out of me.

The saddest part is that I'm still on file with them, despite never having confirmed the address Coleman gave them.

Sunday, June 21

David Coleman must be tripping out on drugs overnight.

Because in the wee hours of the morning, he signed me up at DateYou again. For those keeping score, that marks his 21st such attempt.

He did change things up this time, though. No selfie, but he listed himself as a 40-year-old with a birth date of January 1. Which seemed to attract the attention of a trio of agents looking for a commission.

hey, tell me something about yourself. Your profile is still pretty empty. :) I'd like to know you better, so tell me something. :) xx Cheyanne60

Hey cutie, when did you join this app? You interested in something more than just chatting? Victoria8118

WOW!! you're a real cutie :) and new also ... perfect!!! We need to clear all that up in a nice chat.. get in touch!! I'm excited to hear from you Hanna6088

If they only knew.

Thursday, June 25

David Coleman is still around.

Overnight, he again tried to reset the password for the account he created for me at Chubby Soulmate.

He sure wants to be my soulmate.

But I don't want to be his.

Sunday, June 28

David Coleman just won't go away.

This time, he signed up at Tinder using my email address. Match, chat, date, they say. At least they were good enough to ask for confirmation of the email address before spamming. They also gave me the opportunity to unlink my address from his account, which I did.

At least Coleman is spacing out his attempts and limiting himself to one at a time.

Tuesday, June 30

This afternoon, David Coleman signed me up at SnapSext again.

He even took the time to take and upload a new selfie he took from his sofa. And he really changed things up by using the screen name SincereCorn180 and listing himself as an 18-year-old who was interested in experimenting, threesomes, friends with benefits, online flirting and in-person relationships.

Too bad he didn't do something really radical like use his own email address. Only then would he know that CertainTexture360 visited his profile. And that mirandapanda420, Elizabeth561 and izadyoda0 wanted him to upload more pictures.

As Bugs Bunny would say, what an ultra maroon.

Wednesday, July 1

Late last night, I got another email from Stage One telling me that Coleman successfully signed up for their voice recognition service. Obviously I'm still on file with them. So I sent the following texts to Coleman:

> *Hey Coleman, heard from Stage One again.*
> *Looks like you signed up with voice recognition.*
> *Tell me Coleman, doesn't it bother you that a stranger knows so much about you?*
> *Obviously it doesn't bother you.*
> *Because if it did, you wouldn't keep using that stranger's email address to sign up for all your websites.*
> *You said you don't do drugs, but I don't believe you.*
> *Either that or you're an Alzheimer patient.*

Then I sent the following to their customer service department:

> *Care to explain the logic behind sending your clients' personal information/account details to unverified email addresses?*

This precipitated the following exchange:

Hi David. I want to make sure we address this appropriately. Please send us a DM with more specific details about the situation along with the type of account you're referring to (no account, card, or loan numbers). Thanks. -Cyn

Someone signed up with Stage One using my email address. You asked for verification. I didn't verify it. Yet I'm still getting tons of spam from Stage One giving details of this person's account, including today when you kindly told me he signed up for your voice recognition feature.

I appreciate you bringing this to our awareness, David. To have us look into this matter further, please continue to DM us your full name, phone number, and address (no account numbers). Thanks. -Tiffany

Excuse me???? Perhaps you misunderstood. I am not a Stage One customer. One of your customers gave my email address to Stage One, who continues to spam me with his account information despite the fact that the address remains unverified. Instead of trying to bleed unnecessary personal information out of me, I would suggest talking to someone in charge and get them to stop sending emails with sensitive personal information to unverified addresses.

We want to do some research and see if another customer may have your email address listed under his or her profile. To have us conduct further research, please DM us your full name, contact number, and email address (no account numbers). Thanks. -Tiffany

Clearly, they remain more hung up on me than on fixing their own issues. Perhaps this Tiffany used to work at Larters Bank. Oh well. I had to try. Maybe it will get tongues wagging around there, if for no other reason than to gripe about that miserable SOB who wouldn't cough up his personal information to them.

It should also be noted that Coleman has stopped responding to my texts. I guess he's mad at me and wants me to leave him alone.

I'll be more than happy to leave him alone.

Once he starts leaving me alone.

Thursday, July 2

David Coleman belongs in a locked dementia ward. Where there are no computers and no Internet access.

Overnight, he signed me up at InstantHookup. Which apparently isn't the same as InstantHookups. Too bad for him that they sent me the system-generated user ID and password he needs to get in.

While online trying to delete the account, I learned that he's never had a one-night stand, he's never faked an orgasm, he doesn't find porno movies arousing, he prefers much younger women, he doesn't masturbate, he believes penis size doesn't really matter and he thinks taste is the most important sense other than touch during sex.

Yes, I know *way* too much about this guy.

Sunday, July 12

David Coleman believes in standing up and protecting home ownership.

Today, he signed me up at Home Ownership Matters. Backed by the National Association of Realtors, they provide timely, relevant and useful information about real estate, finance and policy issues for current and prospective home owners. They also advocate for laws and policies that are good for the community and good for neighborhoods.

Too bad they don't advocate for good laws and policies regarding email subscriptions.

Monday, July 13

David Coleman has now taken an interest in trivia.

Today, he signed me up at Trivia Genius. Keep your brain engaged with Trivia Genius, they say.

If only he had a brain to engage.

Which well-known color do some scientists believe may not actually exist was the question posed in the email.

I would like to pose the question as to why they don't ask for confirmation before allowing someone to sign up for their email list.

Wednesday, July 15

David Coleman still wants to further his education.

This evening, he requested information from Florida Career College again. Their medical assistant technician program interests him. They say they'll call him in the next day or so to give him the lowdown on the hands-on learning and the clinical internships they offer along with one-on-one tuition planning.

Except that the number he entered was "col-eman."

Now he can't even get that much right. But he does expect to be able to do blood draws and X-rays.

Right.

So for the hell of it, I sent this off to Coleman:

Hey Coleman, heard from Florida Career College
Looks like you want to be a medical technician
Hard to pass college exams when you keep failing the most important question — what's
your email address?

Thursday, July 16

Another day, another reminder from David Coleman that he's still around.

This evening, I heard from another recruiter at Southeastern Interstate University. The Daffy Duck people. Coleman had requested more information from them once again, but the recruiter has been unable to reach him to discuss how they could help move his education forward.

Nothing they can do could help with his education. Or Daffy's.

Because you can't fix stupid.

Wednesday, July 29

This afternoon, David Coleman got a reminder to respond to the U.S. Census.

It's his once-a-decade opportunity, they say. His community's future will be shaped by his response. And no citizenship questions will be asked.

But like so many other places, they keep asking that ever-present pesky question that he can't answer correctly.

What's your email address?

Tuesday, August 4

Today, I got another promotional mailing from Florida Career College. Even though I had unsubscribed from their mailings after the last one.

Unsubscribe apparently doesn't mean unsubscribe. So I tried again. Maybe this time it will stick.

Tuesday, September 29

David Coleman apparently called Stage One's customer service line yesterday. And Stage One wants to know how it went.

But they must not want to know too badly since they sent the survey asking for feedback to me instead of to Coleman. Which means I'm still on file with them. A sad state of affairs indeed. Even with most of the dating sites Coleman signed me up with, I was able to go in and delete the account. Yet I have no such option with Stage One to get my address off their files. So when they asked, on a scale of 0 to 10, how likely I was to recommend Stage One to a friend or family member, I answered 0 and gave them this comment:

> *That's because I'm not a Stage One customer. Someone else gave my address to Stage One, who asked for verification, never got it, yet keeps my address on file and continues to spam me with the account holder's personal information.*

Thank you for completing the survey, they said at the end. Your feedback is important to us.

Right.

Friday, October 9

Even though David Coleman seems to be receding into my rearview mirror, Kilton University remains as persistent as ever.

This afternoon, another of their admissions counselors spammed me again, giving me a full list of the courses he would need to take to obtain a degree.

From: Helen Barnes
Subject: Criminal Justice. Kilton University
To: David Coleman

David-

Kilton University's Associates of Arts degree in Criminal Justice provides preparation in many areas of the criminal justice system. Topics include but are not limited to: deviant behavior, forensics, law enforcement and investigation, victimology, private security, corrections and juvenile justice and how components work together and are governed by our laws, the Supreme Court and the U.S. Constitution. This exploration of the American criminal justice system culminates with an emphasis on research, analysis and the future of the system.

Can be completed in 20 months. 12 Classes in general Education and 8 Classes in your Major. You have the choice to take all of your classes online or a combination of campus and online. Classes start every month! Join our 10/26 class today.

Regards,

Helen Barnes
Admissions Counselor
Kilton University
College of Advanced Technology

Which prompted another reply, though I'm not sure it will do any good. They're just as thick-headed as Coleman.

Helen, as I've repeatedly told so many of your colleagues, David Coleman of Deland mistakenly gave you my email address. Yet although he seems to have figured out his mistake, the people at Kilton keep bullheadedly insisting on emailing me despite my repeated demands to have my address removed from your files.

So I'll try saying it again. And in clear and plain English.

Please remove my address from your files.

I never want to hear from Kilton University again.

Is this that hard for you and your colleagues to comprehend?

Or are you just intentionally being obnoxious?

Thursday, November 5

I had forgotten that today was David Coleman's birthday. That is, until two of the old dating sites he had signed me up for were kind enough to send birthday greetings. Apparently my email address was still on file with them. Love knows no boundaries, says one of them. The other says they offer a thrilling companionship with romantic and caring women from abroad. More like a thrilling companionship with your credit card.

Sadly, they didn't allow me to delete the accounts, but I was at least able to reroute them to Coleman's real email address. And with any luck, he'll be able to connect with any of the slew of agents whose profiles popped up. Marija asks, "My Mom says that men are always right, is it true?" Divya says she is so lonely and asks, "Can you make me smile?"

Sorry, Divya. Try someone else.

He's Back

Saturday, November 28

David Coleman has seemingly risen from the ashes. Or maybe he just got out of jail.

Over the last three days, he tried two more times to sign up at InstantHookup and made another attempt at InstantHookups. As before, both sites sent me a system-generated user ID and password he needs to get in that he can't possibly guess.

This time, he says he's looking for one-on-one dating, online friends, swingers, alternative activities, fetishes and/or other activity.

All I'm looking for is for him to start using his own email address.

Thursday, December 3

Now David Coleman wants to book an appointment for lab test.

But once again, he gave them my email address instead of his own.

Then again, it's probably just as well. No sense wasting medical resources on him. Because there's no cure for Coleman's biggest health problem.

The lack of a brain.

Sunday, December 19

David Coleman remains a glutton for punishment.

But unfortunately, he's just as intent on sending some of that punishment my way.

Over the last couple of days, he made three more attempts to sign up at InstantHookup. Then he tried twice more at WellHello, a site he hadn't tried in nearly eight months. Of course, he can't access either site since both of them sent me the login credentials. But that never stops him from trying. For good measure, he tried reactivating an old account at another dating site he first signed me up for a year ago August.

How can someone be so dense?

Tuesday, December 22

David Coleman is officially back in the saddle again.

Today, he signed up at four new dating sites. If only he knew that his profile garnered some attention. Oneluv24779 from Miami sent him a message, as did pandorabox69 from Brooksville. Later, NaughtyNites247 also sent him a message. "Secret admirers" Svetlana and Anita wanted him to say hello.

In that profile, he listed his occupation as "security" and said he lived in Opa-locka. Maybe he moved and didn't tell me. The background he used for his selfie looked different. And I hadn't seen him with that white fleece top before. Interestingly, he now claims to drink often. In the past, he'd always referred to himself as a social drinker. Striking out so often on these sites has perhaps driven him to seek solace in the bottle.

Whereas he just said "like sex" and "like to give women head" on the first three sites, he had a different message on the last one. On that site, he stated he was interested in communication with people who have strong family values, who think marriage is important and who want to have fun. And that he still wants more children. As if the world needs more little Colemans running around.

As always, it's pretty tough to communicate with someone when you keep giving out a stranger's email address instead of your own.

Thursday, December 24

In the wee hours of the morning, David Coleman dug into the archives one more time when he again signed me up at DateYou, a site he hadn't visited for six months. Maybe he was on another drinking binge overnight.

He got a couple of responses from their agents. Zelda93 wanted him to write something about himself so she could tell if he was her type. Laurence6437 wanted to know why he was being so secretive since he didn't upload a picture.

But in the end, his 22nd attempt at DateYou didn't go any better than his first 21.

That guy will never learn.

Epilogue

I don't know if I will ever be free of David Coleman. But at least Larters Bank and the many others who Coleman gave my address to have, for the most part, left me alone, having finally gotten it through their thick skulls that I am not David Coleman. Even if I were, God forbid, I'd still have had the right to opt out of their emails, a right they don't respect. Truth of the matter is that I remain just as upset with places like that as I am with Coleman. Coleman is just stupid, whereas legitimate and otherwise reputable companies are supposed to have some professional ethics when it comes to email communication. Ethics that should allow anyone to easily unsubscribe from their emails, or better yet, not receive them at all without verification. Nintendo and Varo (their real names) were among the few good guys in all of this. In fact, I received no more verification requests from Varo after sending them an email asking for my email address to be blocked, likely indicating they took the matter seriously after only one such request. This is in sharp contrast to Larters (not their real name), whom I had to fire off nearly 50 emails to in order to get their attention.

In addition to the hundreds of emails I've received intended directly for Coleman, I continue to live with the residual spam from all the sleazy dating sites he gave my email address to. Fortunately, I've been able to create filters that shunt the vast majority of it to my spam folder or delete it immediately.

To date, he tried to or did sign me up at 218 different websites. By far the largest category is dating with 127. The other popular categories included financial with 35, jobs with 13 and education with 11.

He made multiple attempts at many of those sites. He tried 40 times with Nintendo, followed by 34 at WellHello and another 22 at DateYou, in addition to more than a dozen at Snapchat. I don't have an exact tally with Snapchat as I wasn't keeping a detailed log at the beginning, since there's no way I could possibly have foreseen how long I would be part of Coleman's online life. All told, he's used my email address at least 411 times spread among those 218 sites. That total is far greater than I've used it myself throughout the many years I've had that account.

Even though Coleman still genuinely believes my email address is his, I found it particularly interesting that not only did I never receive any communication from his friends or family, but at no point did he ever try to hack into my account. As I noted earlier, it is also interesting that only on rare occasions did he ever try to reset the password for an account he created that I locked him out of. As it is common for people to forget their password, most websites offer a clearly visible option to reset it, yet it was as if he figured he should just move on if his password inexplicably stopped working. It gave me further insight into Coleman's tiny brain, which seemed utterly incapable of any rational thought. Yet he had enough brain power and determination to find so many dating sites and keep signing up with them despite never being able to verify "his" email address or get any responses. It really did seem as if his was a case of early onset of Alzheimer's or dementia, perhaps mixed in with drug and/or alcohol abuse. Maybe even a case of fetal alcohol syndrome.

I've been able to share some laughs about it all with my friends, but in reality, the whole affair has been anything but funny. The occasional person has mistaken my email address for theirs, but those are just nuisance one-off cases. There are many stories that people have shared online about others using their email address for lengthy periods, but nothing comes close to my experience with Coleman.

Many advise using the so-called "nuclear" option with such a person when all else fails, as I did in locking Coleman out of those accounts or deleting them entirely. When doing so, however, I was always careful to use the Tor browser or a VPN with a no-log policy in order to hide my location. As some of the dating sites sent me the IP address he signed up from, which could have allowed me to track him right to his front door, I could have been similarly tracked from the IP address I used to delete the accounts. Even though Coleman is an imbecile in every respect, you can never be too careful with such things. For all I know, his signup at the U.S. Concealed Carry Association could have been a subtle threat.

Finally, throughout this affair, I had considered alternative ways of getting through to him besides those I described. In addition to filing charges with police for online harassment, another was to hire a lawyer and pursue him through the legal system. I had little doubt that I would have had a strong case and could potentially have won a four- or five-figure judgment against him. But the process would have caused me a lot of grief and in the end, a judgment is just a piece of paper. No one knows better than me that Coleman's net worth is virtually zero, and as they say, you can't get blood from a stone.

That led me to another idea. I drafted a formal demand letter that I was going to print on paper and send through an anonymous mailing service. My thought was to make it sound like it was coming from a lawyer in order to make an impression on him; I added personal details like his full legal name, phone number and date of birth and the full list of websites he had signed up with using my email address so he would know this was legitimate and not some sort of scam. I ultimately decided against it for two reasons. First, using too many big words could have the opposite effect and would go right over his head. After all, Coleman is a simpleton. Second, even if it did make an impression, there was the very real possibility that he still wouldn't have stopped. In that case, it would have obligated me to invoke the long arm of the law, and if I didn't, the whole thing would have come across as an empty threat.

Nonetheless, I share that unsent demand letter here for the benefit of anyone else facing the same or similar circumstances as I did with Coleman.

David Julian Coleman
[address redacted]
Phone: 786-555-7546
Date of Birth: [redacted]

Re: Your unauthorized use of david82@FreeAMail.net.

Sir:

I am the legitimate owner of the email address david82@FreeAMail.net, one that I have actively used for the past decade.

In or about the middle of August of last year, you began signing up to a series of websites using that address. Beginning with Snapchat, you had used that address to attempt to create several bank accounts (Larters Bank, Varo, N26), seek and apply for work (ZipRecruiter, Initiative Trading, CBX Expedited), apply for credit and loans (Bank of America, Capital One, Discover), inquire about and register for programs with technical schools and universities (Central Florida Motorcycle Institute, City College, Parker University Global, Southeastern Interstate University) and sign up with hundreds of online dating forums along with many other sites including Instagram, Nintendo, Domino's Pizza, Storage King and Tobacco Free Florida. To date, you have made a total of 411 attempts and/or contacts at 218 different websites using my email address. Enclosed for your reference is a full list of all those websites.

While you may have initially been mistaken in thinking that address was yours, given that you received no response from any of those sites, no rational person could possibly be unaware of his error. With Nintendo alone, you had made 40 unsuccessful attempts to create an account using that address during the latter half of October and into November. Between October and April, you had made another 32 unsuccessful attempts at the dating site WellHello.com.

I repeatedly contacted you via email and text to alert you that you had been using my email address and to demand you stop doing so. In addition, I had contacted several third parties, including representatives of Varo, Central Florida Motorcycle Institute and Kilton University, institutions with whom you had spoken in order to ask them to try to impress upon you that you were quoting someone else's email address as your own. Yet even though they had indeed done so, you continued to wantonly and recklessly try to build yourself an online identity using an email address that you have to be fully aware is not yours.

Therefore, I demand you **CEASE AND DESIST** from any further use of my email address david82@FreeAMail.net. I further demand you acknowledge receipt of this letter via email to me at david82@FreeAMail.net and in that email, indicate your agreement to comply.

Mr. Coleman, it is my wish to avoid the courts if at all possible. However, if you continue to pursue this destructive pattern of behavior, you will leave me with no alternative but to initiate **civil and criminal proceedings against you**. Your actions have subjected me to incessant online harassment and if forced to launch legal action, I will attempt to recover general and punitive monetary damages for loss of professional reputation and time spent disposing of accounts you have created under my credentials and eradicating my inbox of the avalanche of spam messages that have come as a direct consequence of your callousness.

You would be well advised to consider that your outrageous conduct can and will have **serious legal and financial repercussions**.

Govern yourself accordingly, sir.

About the Author

Born and raised in Winnipeg, Manitoba, Curtis Walker lives in St. Catharines, Ontario. His passions include the history of the original Winnipeg Jets (1972-1996) and the World Hockey Association as well as the New Jersey Generals and the United States Football League.

In addition to his four books on the Jets, Curtis has written many other titles. For more details, visit his website at http://curtiswalker.com/.

www.ingramcontent.com/pod-product-compliance
Lightning Source LLC
LaVergne TN
LVHW051247050326
832903LV00028B/2626